The Morning Star

Vol. 5 ♦ JOURNAL ♦ No. 2

Editor: Rick Joyner
Contributing Editors: Jack Deere, Francis Frangipane, and Dudley Hall
General Editor: Steve Thompson
Managing Editor: Dianne C. Thomas
Heading Design: Vann Dennis, Mark Alan Tunno
Production Manager: Mike Chaille
Production Assistant: Bill Box
Copy Editors: Becky Chaille, Sally Compton, Gloria Samuels

The Morning Star Journal is published quarterly, 4 issues per year, by MorningStar Publications Inc., 16000 Lancaster Hwy, Charlotte, NC 28277-2061. Spring-1995 issue. Second-class postage pending, Charlotte, NC and additional mailing offices.

POSTMASTER: Send address corrections to The Morning Star Journal, 16000 Lancaster Hwy, Charlotte, NC 28277-2061. Subscription Rates: One year $12.95. Outside U.S. $20.00.

MorningStar Publications is a non-profit organization dedicated to the promulgation of important teachings and timely prophetic messages to the church. We also attempt to promote interchange between the different streams, emphases and denominations in the body of Christ.

To receive a subscription to The Morning Star Journal, send payment along with your name and address to MorningStar Publications, 16000 Lancaster Hwy., Charlotte, NC 28277-2061, (704) 542-0278, (1-800-542-0278—Orders only) FAX (704) 542-0280. One year (4 quarterly issues) U.S. $12.95; outside U.S. $20.00. Prices are subject to change without notice.

Reprints. Photocopies of any part of the contents of this publication may be made freely. However, to re-typeset information, permission must be requested in writing from MorningStar Publications, 16000 Lancaster Hwy., Charlotte, NC 28277-2061.

Letters. Direct all correspondence to the address above. Contributions are tax deductible. Your support is appreciated.

THE BEGINNING OF WISDOM

BY RICK JOYNER

All Scriptures NAS unless otherwise noted.

Intimacy with God should be our highest goal. That is our Father's desire. He loved us so much that He sent His only Son to pay the ultimate price so that we can come boldly before His throne. This is certainly the greatest privilege in all of creation—to have access to the Most High God. The whole creation marvels at the Lord's special affinity for man. However, there is an unholy familiarity with God that some fall into which is a most deadly trap. Judas was familiar with Jesus, but John was intimate. There can be a big difference.

Those who dwell in this precarious condition of an unholy familiarity usually reject this kind of exhortation because it causes them to have an uncomfortable fear. However, the Scriptures are clear that if we do not have the proper fear of God we will depart from the path of life. It may well be that the lack of a pure and holy fear of God is the single greatest cause of weakness and sin in the Western church today. **"And by the fear of the LORD one keeps away from evil"** (Proverbs 16:6). **"How blessed is the man who fears [God] always, but he who hardens his heart will fall into calamity"** (Proverbs 28:14).

One of the Bible's most scathing denunciations of the condition of mankind, Romans 3:10-18, is a compilation of quotes from the Old Testament, concluding with the reason for this great corruption: **"THERE IS NO FEAR OF GOD BEFORE THEIR EYES"** (verse 18). Jeremiah equated not having the fear of the Lord with forsaking the Lord:

> **"Your own wickedness will correct you, and your apostasies will reprove you; know therefore and see that it is evil and bitter for you to forsake the LORD your God, and the dread of Me is not in you"** declares the Lord GOD of hosts (Jeremiah 2:19).

Many have a concept that this fear is simply a reverence, or a respect, for God. Certainly that is implied, but we must understand that this is a reverence and respect multiplied to the *highest power*. When either Old or New Covenant saints encountered the living God, we would be hard pressed to call their reactions mere respect or reverence. They were so afraid that they were surprised to have lived through the encounter! When John, the Lord's best friend (who could lean his head upon His breast), near the end of his life encountered the risen Lord, he fell to the ground, **"as a dead man" (Revelation 1:17).** Anyone who does not have a true fear of the Lord has not truly seen Him *as He is.*

As the psalmist declared, **"The fear of the LORD is the beginning of wisdom"** **(Psalm 111:10).** Isaiah said, **"The fear of the LORD is his treasure" (Isaiah 33:6).** Proverbs 2:1-5 links these two important thoughts together in one of the great biblical exhortations:

> **My son, if you will receive my sayings, and treasure my commandments within you,**
>
> **Make your ear attentive to wisdom, incline your heart to understanding;**
>
> **For if you cry for discernment, lift your voice for understanding;**
>
> **If you seek her as silver, and search for her as for hidden treasures;**
>
> ***Then you will discern the fear of the LORD,* and discover the knowledge of God.**

Wisdom is a great treasure. Treasure is not found just lying on the ground, or growing on trees. What makes something a treasure is that it is either rare, or hard to obtain. Wisdom is such a treasure. It is difficult to find and easy to lose. Even Solomon, the wisest man to walk the earth until Wisdom Himself came, lost his wisdom and fell at the end of his life. When we find true wisdom, we will find the fear of the Lord. When we lose the fear of the Lord, we lose wisdom, regardless of how much knowledge or understanding we have.

It is for this reason easy to understand why there is so much confusion about the fear of the Lord. The true grace of the fear of the Lord is rare. Few are willing to pay the price to even seek it, and it is something that we must seek. Wisdom will never come to those who do not seek it, and it will quickly be lost by all who do not properly value it. And the beginning of all wisdom is to properly fear the Lord.

"Anyone who does not have a true fear of the Lord has not truly seen Him as He is."

If you knew for certain that there was a vein of gold hidden in your back yard that could supply all of your needs for the rest of your life, you would be wise to quit your job and lay everything else aside to dig until you found it. However, there is treasure greater than the mother lode lying on many of our bookshelves, often just accumulating dust—the Bible! Spurgeon once lamented that he could find ten men who would die for the Bible for every one who would read it. This could also apply to the other spiritual disciplines. We can probably find ten men who will fight for prayer in public schools for every one who actually prays with his own children at home. We may find ten Christians who complain about the sex and violence on television for every one who actually refuses to watch it. Our power to be salt and light in the world does not depend just on *what* we believe, but on how faithful we are to our beliefs.

Knowing the truth without living it only brings judgment. This is precisely the definition of a hypocrite, for whom the Lord reserved His most vehement condemnation.

We may feel secure in our condition because we have had certain spiritual experiences, or attend church regularly, pay tithes, or submit ourselves to other spiritual disciplines, but the Lord repeatedly warned in His teachings that many who know the truth, and even do great works, will not enter into the kingdom. If we are like the foolish virgins and neglect to keep our vessels full of oil, when He comes we are going to be in a most desperate condition. Those foolish virgins were believers, who were waiting for Him to come. This may be a good time to check and see how much oil is in your own lamp!

"We can probably find ten men who will fight for prayer in public schools for every one who actually prays with his own children at home."

One of the greatest treasures a person can possess is the proper fear of the Lord. All of the other graces and blessings are built upon this foundation. As the Lord explained, **"Where your treasure is, there will your heart be also" (Matthew 6:21).** If we really have a heart to fear the Lord, we will spend our time seeking it. How many of us actually spend more time in front of the television each week, or even reading the newspaper, than we do in studying our Bibles or in prayer?

Many people quit spending as much time reading their Bibles or in prayer simply because they found it so dry they did not feel there was much profit in it. But that is almost certainly how it began for even the greatest Christian preachers. The difference is they had such faith that the treasure was there that they did not quit digging until they found it. Treasure does not lie on the surface, and it will always be difficult to get to. But who esteems its value enough to give what it takes to find it? **"It is the glory of God to conceal a matter, but the glory of kings is to search out a matter" (Proverbs 25:2).**

Many of us, especially in the West, have been spoiled by an easy salvation. This is not to imply that we can do anything to attain salvation, but there are requirements for walking in truth that are seldom preached in the West. For the first three centuries of the church, it usually required the sacrifice, or at least the risk of losing everything that one possessed to become a Christian—including life itself. After the church was institutionalized by the state, those who rejected the dogma of the state institutions of the church often suffered the same persecution, continuing even to the present time in many countries. We should be very thankful for the religious liberty that we now have, but it is very fragile. If we take it for granted it will almost certainly be lost. But even worse than that, if our truth is taken for granted it has already been lost, regardless of how much religious liberty we enjoy.

We have often preached both a salvation and a Christian life that reflect our addiction to convenience, and it can be questioned whether some of our concepts of the Christian life are biblical. Many are tragically being made to feel spiritually comfortable in a condition in which their eternal lives are in jeopardy.

A few years ago I was told by the Lord that the church in America was almost completely unprepared for difficulties, and that great difficulties were coming. I was also told that the times of trouble would not be difficult for those who properly prepared for them. In the years since receiving this word, I have come to understand that this preparation is basically walking in the proper fear of the Lord. Ponder this promise given to those who fear Him:

Surely the Lord GOD does nothing unless He reveals His secret counsel to His servants the prophets (Amos 3:7).

Wouldn't you like to be one of those to whom the Lord reveals His secret counsel before He does anything? Psalm 25:14 says, **"The secret of the LORD is for those who fear Him."** The one characteristic that is profoundly evident in the lives of all of the prophets was their pure and holy fear of the Lord. It could be accurately said that the fear of the Lord is the foundation of the prophetic ministry, and must be evident in all who desire to know the secrets of the Lord.

Behold, the eye of the LORD is upon them that fear him, upon them that hope in his mercy (Psalm 33:18 KJV).

Of course, the Lord knows everything that goes on in the earth, but this phrase— "to have your eye upon someone"— reveals a special affection and care. This same thought is elaborated on in the following psalm:

The angel of the LORD encamps around those who fear Him, and rescues them.

O taste and see that the LORD is good; how blessed is the man who takes refuge in Him!

O fear the LORD, you His saints; for to those who fear Him, there is no want.

The young lions do lack and suffer hunger; but they who seek the LORD shall not be in want of any good thing (Psalm 34:7-10).

The following Scriptures promise rewards much greater than any earthly treasure we could accumulate. I encourage you to read them patiently and let them stir your heart to desire the fear of the Lord, that you might properly seek Him.

Thou hast given a banner to those who fear Thee, that it may be displayed because of the truth.

That Thy beloved may be delivered (Psalm 60:4-5).

For Thou hast been a refuge for me, a tower of strength against the enemy.

Let me dwell in Thy tent forever; let me take refuge in the shelter of Thy wings.

For Thou hast heard my vows, O God; thou hast given me the inheritance of those who fear Thy name (Psalm 61:3-5).

Surely His salvation is near to those who fear Him, that glory may dwell in our land (Psalm 85:9).

For as high as the heavens are above the earth, so great is His lovingkindness [mercy] toward those who fear Him.

Just as a father has compassion on his children, so the LORD has compassion on those who fear Him (Psalm 103:11, 13).

He will fulfill the desire of those who fear Him; He will also hear their cry and save them (Psalm 145:19).

The LORD favors those who fear Him, those who wait for His lovingkindness (Psalm 147:11).

The fear of the LORD prolongs life (Proverbs 10:27).

In the fear of the LORD there is strong confidence, and his children will have refuge.

The fear of the LORD is a fountain of life, that one may avoid the snares of death (Proverbs 14:26-27).

Better is a little with the fear of the LORD, than great treasure and turmoil with it (Proverbs 15:16).

The fear of the LORD leads to life, so that one may sleep satisfied, untouched by evil (Proverbs 19:23).

The reward of humility and the fear of the LORD are riches, honor and life (Proverbs 22:4).

"But for you who fear My name the sun of righteousness will rise with healing in its wings; and you will go forth and skip about like calves from the stall.

And you will tread down the wicked, for they shall be ashes under the soles of your feet on the day which I am preparing," says the LORD of hosts (Malachi 4:2-3).

Have you noticed that many of the popular "claim it" promises are conditional upon us having the fear of the Lord? Could this be why many people spend countless hours memorizing the promises and quoting them without result? Have you noticed how some even use these promises to dictate orders to the Lord? Does that reflect the proper fear of the Lord? Presumption often has the appearance of authority, but it is a profound folly.

We can have a pure heart for the Lord, and yet still walk in the folly of presumption, just as King David did when he tried to bring the ark of God to Jerusalem (see II Samuel 6:1-11). The ark represents the glory of God's manifest presence. David assumed that he could move the ark on a new ox cart. Assumption is a basic characteristic of presumption, and those who assume often are lacking in a basic respect for authority. The ox represents carnal strength, and there are many who believe they can bring in the glory of God with their own strength and wisdom, though they would never put it in those terms. That presumption is not just foolish—it is deadly!

Uzzah was a faithful and good man. He obviously had a heart for the Lord, too. When the ox cart was nearly upset, Uzzah reached out his hand to steady the ark. That would seem like a very noble thing to do, but the anger of the Lord burned against Uzzah so that He struck him dead! Uzzah means "strength," and he thought that he could in his own strength steady the glory of God—a terrible presumption for which he paid with his life. Even so, David had set the stage for such a catastrophe by the way he had tried to bring the ark to Jerusalem.

"God has never lost an election because He does not even run in them."

David first became angry, and then he got wise: **"So David was afraid of the LORD that day; and he said, 'How can the ark of the LORD come to me?' "** **(verse 9).** It was wise of David to fear the Lord. It was also wise of him not to give up because of this one mistake, even though it was so tragic.

The Lord is pouring out His Spirit today like I have not seen Him do in over two decades. There are many "Davids" who have sought Him and have a great passion to see His glory returned to the church, and the Lord wants to come. However, many are succumbing to the same mistake that David made. The casualness, and even arrogance, with which some have begun to handle His presence are preparing the way for terrible consequences if there is not quick repentance.

After the outbreak of the Lord's anger at Perez-uzzah, David stopped everything to seek the Lord until he was told the way that the ark was to be moved. He brought the priests who would carry the ark according to the prescribed manner. Then, instead of trying to use the ox to bring Him to Jerusalem, David sacrificed an ox and a fatling every six paces (verse 13). We will never bring the glory of the Lord to the church by our own strength. If we are wise we will sacrifice to the Lord whatever strength we have, just as Paul exhorted:

> **I urge you therefore, brethren, by the mercies of God, to present your bodies a living and holy sacrifice, acceptable to God, which is your spiritual service of worship.**
>
> **And do not be conformed to this world, but be transformed by the renewing of you mind, that you may prove what the will of God is, that which is good and acceptable and perfect.**
>
> **For through the grace given to me I say to every man among you not to think more highly of himself than he ought to think; but to think so as to have sound judgment, as God has allotted to each a measure of faith (Romans 12:1-3).**

Trusting the Arm of Flesh

It is a blessing of God on a nation to have good leaders, and it is a curse to have bad ones. However, it is also apostasy to "trust in the horses and chariots."

> **Woe to those who go down to Egypt for help, and rely on horses, and trust in chariots because they are many, and in horsemen because they are very strong, but they do not look to the Holy One of Israel, nor seek the LORD! (Isaiah 31:1).**

It is a telltale symptom of the church's condition that great despair came upon Christians with the election of a liberal president, and that hope returned with the conservative victory in 1994. I personally agree much more with the conservative platform, and I always vote conservative unless I feel specifically directed by the Lord to do otherwise. Even so, I know that the glory of God is not going to come to our country because of an election. Even though we all want to see the glory of God fall on this land, how we seek to bring it about is crucial.

Good legislation is important, but it is not nearly as important, or as effective, as the church when she walks in the spiritual authority she has been given. If the church gave as much attention to prayer and the proper fear of the Lord, we would not even need much of the legislation that now seems so important. If righteousness could come by legislation it would be as shallow and as weak as the men who would take credit for it. What the Lord is about to do will not be credited to men, regardless of their position.

> **You are not to say, "It is a conspiracy!" in regard to all that this people call a conspiracy, and you are not to**

fear what they fear or be in dread of it.

It is the LORD of hosts whom you should regard as holy. *And He shall be your fear, and He shall be your dread. Then He shall become a sanctuary* (Isaiah 8:12-14).

When we have the true and holy fear of the Lord, we do not have to fear anything else on this earth. To have the true fear of the Lord is evidenced by our not fearing what the world fears. God has never lost an election because He does not even run in them. His policy in our country will not be handed down from Washington. But those who have authority with God through prayer, can dictate policy in Washington, regardless of who is in the office. **"For the LORD is our judge, the LORD is our lawgiver, the LORD is our king" (Isaiah 33:22).** Here we see that the Lord *is* all three branches of government.

When the church becomes like Daniel, fearing Him more than man, God will then deal with our government like He did Nebuchadnezzar's. Even this man (who was far more ruthless than the propagandized Saddam Hussein), who destroyed Jerusalem, the temple, and then built a great golden idol to himself, who would on a whim destroy multitudes, still bowed his knee when He saw the power of the God of Daniel. When we, like Daniel, refuse to defile ourselves with the food and drink of the heathen and to worship their idols, but instead worship the Lord openly regardless of the consequences, He will then give us wisdom and power that will confound the heathen, and cause them to bow the knee to our God.

See to it that you do not refuse Him who is speaking. For if those did not escape when they refused him who warned them on earth, much less shall we escape who turn away from Him who warns from heaven.

And His voice shook the earth then, but now He has promised, saying, "YET ONCE MORE I WILL SHAKE NOT ONLY THE EARTH, BUT ALSO THE HEAVEN."

And this expression, "Yet once more," denotes the removing of those things which can be shaken, as of created things, in order that those things which cannot be shaken may remain.

Therefore, since we receive a kingdom which cannot be shaken, let us show gratitude, by which we may offer to God an acceptable service with reverence and awe;

FOR OUR GOD IS A CONSUMING FIRE (Hebrews 12:25-29).

We are heirs to a kingdom that cannot be shaken, regardless of elections, wars, revolutions, or even natural disasters. If we shake when the world shakes it is because we are building on the wrong foundation.

Therefore thus says the Lord GOD, "Behold, I am laying in Zion a stone, a tested stone, a costly cornerstone for the foundation, firmly placed. *He who believes in it [Him] will not be disturbed"* (Isaiah 28:16).

For a child will be born to us, a son will be given to us; and the government will rest on His shoulders; and His name will be called Wonderful Counselor, Mighty God, Eternal Father, Prince of Peace.

There will be no end to the increase of His government or of peace, on the throne of David and over his kingdom, to establish it and to

uphold it with justice and righteousness from then on and forevermore. The zeal of the LORD of hosts will accomplish this (Isaiah 9:6-7).

It is right for us to want good, righteous government. But it can be wrong as to how we go about trying to bring it in. This is not to negate our proper duty to vote, possibly even standing up for certain candidates. However, when we are either overly disturbed or overly relieved because of the results of an election, it shows that we are placing our hope in men rather than in the Lord. The best of men can fall, and the worst men can be used for good by the Lord.

"The power of the church does not lie in her ability to articulate the truth, but to walk in it."

We must Believe in Our Hearts, Not Just Our Minds

"That which is born of flesh is flesh, and that which is born of the Spirit is spirit" (John 3:6). We are utterly dependent on the Holy Spirit for bearing true spiritual fruit. Because the Holy Spirit is "the Spirit of truth," He will only endorse with His presence and power that which is true. The Lord judges our hearts, not just our minds. For this reason "heart religion" is about to take precedence over "intellectual religion." However, we must never abandon our commitment to sound biblical truth. The power soon to be released in the church will be through those who have embraced both the Word and the Spirit.

The great darkness that is now sweeping the world has erupted on our watch. The coming great release of power in Christian leadership will be the result of a great repentance and conviction of sin that sweeps over the body of Christ. Movements that exhort men and women to faithfulness and their spiritual responsibilities will have a profound impact on the whole church. The repentance that has resulted from the humiliations of the last decade are also about to bear great fruit.

As the Lord declared, **"And whoever exalts himself shall be humbled; and whoever humbles himself shall be exalted" (Matthew 23:12).** Even though much of the humility has been the result of judgment, the degree to which the church has embraced the judgment has prepared her to be lifted up in the esteem of the nations. Even though the attacks and slander will always be with us, the world's esteem for the advancing church is about to rise.

Patience Bears Lasting Fruit

Some consider it a travesty that the New Testament does not take a decisive stand against some of the great moral evils of the times in which it was written, such as slavery, abortion and infanticide (the practice of killing babies if they were not the desired sex, or had defects). It is true that the first century leaders of the church did not engage in frontal assaults against these great evils. However, it was not because of negligence or irresponsibility; they had a higher strategy with a greater power. They did not just flail at the branches of human depravity—they put the ax to the root of the tree. Neither did they try to accomplish the purpose of God in their own strength, or by using an "ox cart."

With focused, unyielding concentration, the apostles of the early church maintained their frontal assault on sin. They drove back the spirit of death by lifting up the Prince of Life. When the issue of slavery did arise in his letter to Philemon, Paul did not attack the issue of slavery directly, but rose above it by appealing to love and the fact that Onesimus was a brother. A man would not make a slave of his brother. This may offend the penchant for militancy that issue-oriented activists usually have, but it is the way of the Spirit. As even the secular historian Will Durant observed, "Caesar tried to change men by changing institutions. Christ changed institutions by changing men."

The goal of the Spirit is to penetrate beyond what a frontal assault on issues can usually accomplish. There are times for bold confrontations, but usually the Lord works much slower than we are willing to accept. This is because He is working toward a much deeper, more complete change— working from the inside out, not the outside in.

"Divinely powerful weapons are about to be reclaimed and used on an unprecedented scale by the church."

Divinely powerful weapons are about to be reclaimed and used on an unprecedented scale by the church. As intercessory and spiritual warfare movements continue to mature, the results will become increasingly spectacular. Even so, the most powerful weapon given to the church is *spiritual truth*. Facts can be "truth," but spiritual truth is only found when knowledge is properly combined with life, which the Holy Spirit can then endorse. It is when we live what we believe that we embrace spiritual, eternal truth. As the church begins to live the truth that she knows, her light will increase and shine into the darkness.

Light is more powerful than darkness. When you open your curtains at night darkness does not come in, but rather light shines out into the darkness. Love is more powerful than either hatred or apathy; life is more powerful than death. As we begin to walk in the light, love and life of the Son of God, we will put darkness and death to flight. The power of the church does not lie in her ability to articulate the truth, but to walk in it. This is the foundation of the great release of power coming to the church.

The Greater Wisdom

The way of the Spirit is practical. He does want the will of God to be done on earth as it is in heaven. We, too, must be committed to seeing practical fruit by practical means. However, our desire not to be so heavenly minded that we do not do any earthly good has often resulted in our becoming so earthly minded that we are not doing any spiritual good. If we impact men spiritually it will ultimately result in earthly good, but the reverse is not true. If we only impact institutions and outward behavior, we may change the facade of things, but we have not dealt with the roots and they will sprout again.

It is not just bearing fruit that counts, but bearing fruit that remains. For us to bear the fruit that is eternal we must learn patience. We are exhorted to be, **"imitators of those who through faith *and* patience inherit the promises" (Hebrews 6:12).** The great wisdom that is about to come upon the church is to see first from the eternal perspective, which will impart the essential ability to plan with strategy and vision for lasting fruit. ■

A WORLD UNDER SIEGE

BY
DUDLEY HALL

All Scriptures NAS unless otherwise noted.

In a society that has denied the Creator, disregarded His boundaries and mocked His kingdom, the walls are down and the enemy has laid siege. There are problems that seem to have no solutions. People are hurting and the old institutions can't meet their needs. There is a story in Scripture that speaks directly to our situation.

In II Kings chapter 6, Israel was having trouble with the Arameans. The Arameans had been enemies of Israel, off and on, for years. Sometimes Israel would join up with the Arameans to fight their brothers in Judah, and sometimes Judah would join up with them and fight against Israel. They were not part of God's covenant people and they were always causing problems for Israel.

This was in the time of Elisha, the prophet and Benhadad, king of Aram. Benhadad had sent his army to besiege Samaria. This caused a great famine in Samaria because they were surrounded by an army which had cut off their water and food supply.

Now it came about after this, that Ben-hadad king of Aram gathered all his army and went up and besieged Samaria.

And there was a great famine in Samaria; and behold, they besieged it, until a donkey's head was sold for eighty shekels of silver, and a fourth of a kab of dove's dung for five shekels of silver (II Kings 6:24-25).

Israel was eating donkeys' heads and dove's dung. There are some interpreters who feel this is too crude and attempt to explain that dove's dung was a term used to describe a wild vegetable. Most have agreed, however, that what they were really eating was dove's dung because there are many instances of that kind of thing happening during a siege.

Let this situation get into your heart so you understand how desperate things were for Israel. The story continues with the king passing by and hearing a woman crying out for help. As he listened two women were arguing about eating their children. The king became so angry at Elisha that he sent a messenger to tell him that this famine was from the Lord and that Elisha needed to die. Elisha was talking with some people when the king's messenger arrived. Elisha said:

> **Listen to the word of the LORD; thus says the LORD, "Tomorrow about this time a measure of fine flour shall be sold for a shekel, and two measures of barley for a shekel, in the gate of Samaria" (II Kings 7:1).**

The day before, a donkey's head was sold for eighty shekels of silver (which is several pounds of silver). A half pint of dove's dung sold for *five* shekels of silver. Elisha was telling them that tomorrow they would be able to buy all the flour and barley they could carry for two-fifths of an ounce of silver. The king's messenger mocked Elisha and the word of the Lord scoffing that, **"if the LORD should make windows in heaven, could this thing be?"** Elisha declared; **"Behold you shall see it with your own eyes, but you shall not eat of it" (verse 2).**

Meanwhile, there were four leprous men at the gate of Samaria. They decided they had nothing to lose, they were going to die of hunger anyway, so why not try the Arameans and see if they could obtain food. As they went to the Arameans' camp to get some food, the Lord made a great sound of horses and the Arameans thought the King of Israel had hired the Hittites and Egyptians to fight against them. The Arameans fled the camp, leaving everything they had behind. The four leprous men entered the camp to find it empty. They ate and drank from one tent to the next. They gathered and hid gold and silver, then returned to the city to share the good news with the people.

"We live in a society, both religious and secular, where pain is outlawed. God's purpose for existing is to deliver us from pain or He is no God at all."

The king was sceptical, but sent a couple of chariots with horses to check out the Arameans' camp. It was just as the leprous men had said. The messenger returned to tell the king and the people went and plundered the camp of the Arameans. As the royal officer who had said God couldn't open the windows of heaven and bring His word to pass was leaning on his staff, the people began to rush around gathering food and he was trampled. He saw the miracle just as Elisha had spoken, but didn't get to experience it for himself.

This story—about a city under a siege which brought famine and confusion—is a prophetic parallel to our nation, people, and even the church. We, too, are under a siege of the enemy.

For instance, in the Dallas/Ft. Worth Metroplex, people walk around in their yards fearful of drive-by shootings. People cannot afford to let their children walk to school even if they live only a block away for fear that they will be picked up by some child molester. We have gangs multiplying against all the efforts of the police and community. Meanwhile, the church continues to work on her programs and to talk about her growth, but I am not sure that we are not selling donkeys' heads and dove's dung.

Modern Day Donkeys' Heads and Dove's Dung

Israel could live for a while on donkeys' heads and dove's dung. It was not real appetizing, but they could survive on it. You pay a lot for a donkey's head and dove's dung when a famine is going on. In our famine society has offered drugs to people, and they've paid the high price of addiction. They've been offered the excitement of illicit sex, and they've paid the high price of AIDS and homosexual perversion.

While our society has offered these remedies, the church has also been selling some offensive things, too, and ours is possibly worse. We've offered them a religion of selfishness. We've been selling the donkey's head of right-wing, red-neck religion. It says to people, "Deny your feelings, deny your pain, ignore your unanswered questions and just follow the rules. Be obedient to the selective requirements of external religion and everything will be all right. Make sure you are doctrinally correct and all your religious acts are properly done. Don't let mysteries and unexplained things get in your way."

The logical conclusion when problems do arise is—good people have good kids, bad people have bad kids and there are no exceptions. There is some security in that for awhile, but it doesn't really come close to biblical Christianity, nor is it anything that God would have us to embrace. Yet this is only one piece of the dung that we have been selling while paying a high price for it—angry disillusionment.

Selfish Self-Consciousness

On the other hand there is the dove's dung of psychological self-investigation, where we must have an answer to everything. *Why* did Mrs. Bobbitt cut off her husband's penis? Not did she do it, but why did she do it? *Why* do I not feel good about myself? *Why* is my self-esteem low? *Why* am I not able to establish self-preserving boundaries so that I have a sense of well-being? *Why* am I not able to express myself

openly and fully? We have left no place for mysteries and no place for pain.

We live in a society, both religious and secular, where pain is outlawed. God's purpose for existing is to deliver us from pain or He is no God at all. We believe that if we experience pain we must be doing something wrong. We also feel that if we have pain, then God somehow owes it to us to intervene and take it away. I submit that without pain we are passionless. It is in the struggle of pain that we learn to trust a good God and our passions are released.

Fear of Pain

Make no mistake, I'm not *for* pain. I'd like to live without it. But I am challenged by the heroes of faith outlined in Hebrews chapter eleven. I have a feeling that every one of those heroes, had they had a choice, would have gone without pain. But they were unwilling to sacrifice their walk with God for a lifestyle that eliminated pain.

Blame God

The people in Samaria wanted to blame God for their situation. The king, in his grief and sorrow, was still responsible for a nation of people who were under siege. He saw the pain as he watched mothers argue over who was going to boil whose baby next. His response was, "I'm going to cut off Elisha's head."

That is many people's solution to our present-day situation—it's God's fault and all those who represent God are at fault. In fact, that is always man's first tendency, "God, why did You let it happen? Why did You let my kid get run over? Why do You let the innocent get mistreated? Why did the tornado hit that house? Why did that person get cancer? It's Your fault, God."

Many people arrogantly say, "I'm not going to believe in a God who lets this kind of stuff happen." Think! You can't have it both ways! Many say man is sovereign and determines what happens in his life. But then when things go wrong they automatically shift the blame to God.

This basic trust issue started in the Garden of Eden. The devil said to Eve, "God cannot truly be trusted. He is not as good as you think He is. You see, He's holding something back from you—you can't eat from that tree over there. He's just being selfish. He doesn't want you to find full self-expression, because if you ever eat of the tree of the knowledge of good and evil you are going to find full self-expression and know all the mysteries of life." When Eve doubted the goodness of God, she sinned along with Adam, by her own choice. From that moment we have inherited a tendency to doubt the goodness of God, especially when there is not much physical evidence to the contrary.

God's Agenda Is Jesus

George McDonald has said, "Has it ever crossed your mind that the only reason you were put on this earth was to know Jesus?" I don't believe we totally understand how much God has set the agenda of the world around Jesus Christ. The Scripture explains that God is going to sum everything up in Jesus. He has given Him a name that is above every name. When our eyes really open we are going to find out that all reality is summed up in Jesus Christ, and that God's whole agenda is to magnify Him. Wouldn't it be smart to be living by that agenda right now? Not an agenda of self-discovery, but an agenda of God-discovery. God wants us to know Him. And *He* is fully

explained in Jesus Christ and there is nothing more important than knowing Him.

Finding Me in Him

If the plan is to know Christ, then where is He? He's in you and He's also in heaven. In Colossians 3:2-3 it says, **"Set your mind on the things above . . . [where] your life is hidden with Christ in God."** We are with Christ who is hidden in God in the heavenlies. Where are the heavenlies? It is the spiritual realm. The kingdom of God as a reality is as present right here and now as you and I are, but it's a reality greater than natural physical reality. When Jesus came and preached that the kingdom of heaven was here, He wasn't talking about up in the clouds somewhere. He was speaking of a reality right here and now. We don't have to go anywhere to be in it, but we do have to repent. Repenting means we have to change our way of thinking.

We have to look at a different screen. There is a different picture. The Scripture tells us to get our minds in the heavenlies where our lives are hidden with Christ in God. When we start discovering who we are in Him and that His glory is tied up with our glory and that His revelation is tied up with our revelation, then we will understand Colossians 3:4: **"When Christ, who is our life, is revealed, then you also will be revealed with Him in glory."**

We will never really understand ourselves until He is totally revealed. We are erroneously looking for eternal answers in a temporal world. If we want to learn about ourselves we should learn about who Christ is, and who we are in Him. The more we know about Him, the more we know about ourselves. Also, the more we know about Him, the less we will need to know about ourselves. As long as our focus is on ourselves, it can't be on Him. Then we are moving from one degree of misery to another. But when our focus is on Him, we are moving from one degree of glory to another (see II Corinthians 3:18). God loves us too much to let us spend our lives thinking about ourselves. In fact, Jesus died on the cross so that we could quit thinking about ourselves. Instead, think about Him—Who is the sum of all things spiritually, in Whom God will sum up all things. What a great day of discovery it will be when Jesus is fully revealed.

Siege of Selfishness

The siege of selfishness has caused a famine in our land. The church has not helped matters by selling donkeys' heads and dove's dung to the people. We have been talking about harvest for years; in fact, I'm still talking about it and I'm still believing for it. Right now, I feel like we are being pushed to the brink of something. A big rain is coming and we are getting the a few drops just before the hard rain. But there is a tendency on our part to put off until tomorrow the victories God has already made available to us today. I do believe something big is about to happen worldwide. When it does, it's going to happen for this reason—SOMEBODY IS GOING TO BELIEVE THAT IT'S ALREADY HERE. There is a time to realize the "now" of faith and experience the present glory of God. We do not need to put everything off until the second coming of Jesus!

I do believe in the Second Coming and I'm looking forward to it for many reasons. First, the dark glass mentioned in I Corinthians 13 is going to be removed and we will see clearly. I want to see the Lord in His full glory and just watch the transformation in us that happens as a result.

Second, Jesus is going to come and establish righteousness in a way that we've never understood it—all injustice will be gone. Somebody said it like this, "Every good thing in this world is an appetizer of what's in eternity. We, however, are trying to make a meal on the appetizer." We have tried to acquire all of life's good things—peace, well-being, self-acceptance, cars, houses and everything else. We get all of these things and yet are still hungry because there is something eternal in us that will not be satisfied until the culmination of His kingdom when all is exposed and revealed. C. S. Lewis said it something like this: "If I have desires that nothing in this world will satisfy, it should be my clue that I wasn't designed just for this world." I understand that eternal call, that hope for the full revelation. I am looking forward to the second coming of Christ, but I am also excited about His first coming. Until His second coming, I believe we are supposed to embrace everything that was accomplished in His first coming.

Back to the Story . . .

In the midst of the situation in Samaria, seemingly for no reason at all, God gave Elisha a word. The city wasn't repenting and they were not locked in all-night prayer meetings. They were in a famine and the king was blaming God, saying, "I am looking for Elisha and I'm going to cut his head off." That's not exactly great repentance. But in the midst of this whole scenario God gives a word to Elisha: "This time tomorrow you will be selling all you can carry for two quarters." Our problem today is the same as their's—GOOD NEWS IS HARD TO BELIEVE.

The king's messenger was as distraught as the king, watching women boil their children and watching people eat dove's dung and donkeys' heads. When Elisha gave this word, the messenger stood there and laughed, thinking, "This couldn't happen even if God opened the windows of heaven." That seems to be a prevalent attitude of people toward God—even people with real problems. If we were sexually abused, grew up in a dysfunctional family, lived in co-dependent relationships, have addiction(s), have cancer, are jobless or homeless, we have real problems. They are not imaginary. These are real problems. However, we tend to believe that God can't fix our problems. We stand like the king's official and laugh, "Ha! If God were to open the windows of heaven—that couldn't happen. You just can't fix that kind of stuff." But they can be fixed.

Paul made this declaration to the believers in Corinth concerning the power of the cross:

> **For the word of the cross is to those who are perishing foolishness, but to us who are being saved it is the power of God.**
>
> **For it is written; "I WILL DESTROY THE WISDOM OF THE WISE, AND THE CLEVERNESS OF THE CLEVER I WILL SET ASIDE."**
>
> **Where is the wise man? Where is the scribe? Where is the debater of this age? Has not God made foolish the wisdom of the world?**
>
> **For since in the wisdom of God the world through its wisdom did not come to know God, God was well-pleased through the foolishness of the message preached to save those who believe.**
>
> **For indeed Jews asked for signs, and Greeks searched for wisdom;**
>
> **but we preached Christ crucified, to Jews a stumbling block, and to Gentiles foolishness,**
>
> **but to those who are the called, both Jews and Greeks, Christ the power of God and the wisdom of God (I Corinthians 2:18-24).**

It's the power of God, not only to the lost who are getting saved and getting their names written in the Book of Life, but also to those who are in the *process* of being saved. The preaching of the cross is the power of God.

Paul thought the preaching of the cross "fixed" folks. I know we don't understand all about the cross, but the further I go in my walk with Jesus the more I understand when Paul said, "I choose not to brag about anything except the cross." I believe I understand a little more about what he meant. The only thing that matters is the new creation that comes out of the cross.

For many of us, the cross is still just a physical thing. We consider it an event in history where Jesus died cruelly with great physical agony. We understand that by His death somehow mysteriously, supernaturally, spiritually our sins were paid for. But I don't think we understand the power of the crucified Christ as it relates to us. The simplicity of it is this: *Jesus came as our representative. He actually lived, died on a cross and paid the penalty for our sins so that we don't ever have to be guilty before God again.* He not only paid for our sins but, in a way that I don't understand, He reached into the future as far as was necessary and brought us into Him so that when He died on the cross, our "self," as a separate entity apart from God, died with Him. All of the scars, the pains and everything consequential to the fall of Adam died on the cross. All of our pasts, with all complexities, all of our fears, everything that came from the fall of man died with Jesus at the cross and was buried with Him. When He came out of the grave, in a way that my natural mind can't understand, we came out with Him, experiencing total freedom from the past. We are new creations because of the cross. He died once to sin but He lives now unto God in righteousness, which gives us a choice of who we really are.

Living with the Truth of the Cross Daily

Does this mean that we won't struggle with something from now on? No, it means that we've got an answer and a solution. The solution is not trying to understand the intricacies of a problem, the solution is believing that there is a higher reality which is in Christ Jesus.

If this message is true (and it is!), then why doesn't the church preach it? Because it's too good to be true. Because the theologians and the philosophers stand leaning on their canes saying, "Ha, God would have to open a window in heaven for that. You can't fix problems like that with a little old simple message about somebody dying on a cross two thousand years ago." Paul said the preaching of the cross would mystify the world, that it would be a stumbling block. But we can believe in Jesus Christ who is a life-giving spirit *today*, who died for us and is resurrected—*today*.

What Is "Getting Well"?

People tell me, "I want to get well; I just want to get well!" What do they mean by getting well? They say, "I want to quit having such low self-esteem. I want to quit being run over by other people. I want to quit having co-dependent relationships. I want to quit being dysfunctional. I want to be spiritually mature (which could be the religious component to the drive of self-improvement)." These things are not bad in themselves, but "getting well" encompasses much more than overcoming a few hangups.

Getting well is really getting so hooked-up with Jesus Christ that we spend the rest of our lives trusting in Him. When we get well we trust Him when our hearts are breaking; we trust Him when there are tears in our eyes; we trust Him when we don't have an answer to our questions. When we get well we trust Him when there is no visible solution to our problems but we trust Him because His life is the only "fix" for our lives. *That's getting well— addicted to trusting Jesus, with many mysteries yet to be revealed.*

Preaching the cross terrorizes Satan because it says that if you are disqualified then you are qualified. Satan spends all of his time trying to disqualify you, causing you to sin, accusing you, putting you under condemnation, making you feel like a jerk, magnifying your low self-esteem. He will continue destroying you until one day you hear the message that Jesus died for folk like you. The cross is only applicable to disqualified folks, so you qualify.

As in our story, if you are a leper and you've been cast out of the city and you are dirty and broke, you are the one that will find the spoil. However, many of us have bought into a Satan-defined mentality and are afraid of the cross.

Nothing to Lose

You may ask, "What's the worst thing that can happen to me if I trust God?" Well, you could die. Then you would have nothing to lose. That's where you must be before the cross makes any sense. God's looking for an army of folks with nothing to lose. Those are the only ones who can overcome the enemy. In Revelation 12:11 it says, **"they overcame him by the blood of the Lamb, and by the word of their testimony; and they loved not their lives unto the death"** (KJV). They had nothing to lose.

Aren't you in the same place? Is this your thought process: "I can't fix it myself. I can't get the Arameans to leave on my own. I can't go back and change my past. I can't make people act right. I tried. I really have tried. I tried to control them. I tried to make decisions for my kids, but I can't. So I have nothing to lose. I don't have any reputation to lose. So, I'll trust God."?

What have you got to lose? Are you still not there? Are you still saying, "I'm going to try a little more, I've got a few more solutions I'm going to try." Remember this, when you get tired of donkeys' heads and dove's dung and you are willing to trust God you will find the spoils are ready for you.

Missing the Good News

There is one other aspect of this story we should address:

When those four lepers found all of the stuff, their first tendency, which fits us today, was to use it on themselves. They found bread, rich food, good wine, all kinds of delicacies and riches, more than they needed. What did they do? They started absorbing it themselves. Putting it in their pockets, hiding it, taking it from one tent to another and hiding it under the bushes. They were saying, "Have we got a deal here!" That's always man's tendency.

Could this be the reason most spiritual movements stop moving? I believe the charismatic movement was a genuine move of God, but what have we done with it? God showed us the beauty of gifts and the body's relationships and the fact that He was a "blessing" God not a "cursing" God. We took that stuff ourselves and stuffed it into our pockets, then used all the gifts on each other.

I believe in all of the expressions of God, but they were not given to us to play with and hide under our bushes. There is a city out there under siege. The government is not going to fix the hurting people. The institutional church is not going to fix them. But some beggar, who knows he is disqualified, will find God. He will discover God loves the disqualified. He will then be willing to take that bread back to town and say, "Look what I've got."

But just as with Israel, the multitude will not go out to see for themselves. They are going to send a little committee and check it out. They probably are just waiting to catch us one more time because it's too good to be true. We all need to face it and just get over it. Just keep standing there full of the life-giving Spirit of Jesus and asking, "Does this look like dove's dung to you? You've got your plate of dove's dung and I've got bread from heaven—which do you want?" If we will declare it and demonstrate it—God will reveal it and redeem it. ■

Dudley Hall is the President of Successful Christian Living Ministries in Euless, Texas. He is the author of *Out of the Comfort Zone—The Church in Transition*. His latest book is *Grace Works— Letting God Rescue You from Empty Religion*. Both books can be ordered from MorningStar Publications.

WINNING THE BATTLE IN THE TRENCHES

BY REGGIE WHITE
with Rick Joyner

All Scriptures NAS unless otherwise noted.

As a defensive lineman in professional football, my primary field of play is in what we call "the trenches." During the game most of the attention is on the quarterback, running backs and receivers, and the mighty struggle going on between the offensive and defensive lines seldom gets noticed. However, every coach will tell you that it is here where most of the games are really won or lost.

Every successful coach builds his team on a foundation of *devotion to fundamentals*—basic blocking and tackling, especially along the line of scrimmage. The best quarterback will not have the opportunity to succeed unless he has a good line to give him the time he needs. The best running back will not get very far without an offensive line that can open holes for him to run through. The team that can control the line of scrimmage will almost always win the game.

These same principles apply in the church. Most of the attention may be on the pastor, evangelists, or music ministries, but the real battle that will determine the success of any church will be in the everyday lives of ordinary believers. The degree of our leaders' and our own success will usually be determined by how well we practice and develop the fundamentals of the faith.

In a football game a defensive lineman has to constantly contend with three main problems: being blindsided, watching for "crack-back" blocks, and fighting off being double- or triple-teamed. Being blindsided is like smiling at your best friend, dropping your guard, and then having him hit you square in the face. Being blindsided is even worse when you are anticipating making contact as the "hitter," and you end up the "hittee."

A "crack-back" block is when an offensive receiver goes in motion toward the opposite side of the field as if he is going to run a pass pattern. The defensive lineman forgets about him because he is out of sight, but he turns back and hits from the blind side. "Crack-back" blocks can result in serious injury, and can even end a football player's career in a split second.

Every Christian has probably experienced such "crack-back" blocks and blindsides from the enemy. He is always trying to hit us on our blind side. Attacks often come from unexpected sources. The devil is not interested in doing what is fair, but what will knock us out of the game. The only protection that a football player has against such tactics is to be in the best shape possible, to increase his field of vision, and to depend on his teammates to help watch his blind side. As Christians we must do the same. The better shape that we are in spiritually the less likely we are to get hurt if we get blindsided. We must also work on increasing our field of vision and being more aware spiritually of what is going on around us. We must also count on our brothers and sisters to watch our blind sides where we cannot see—and we all do have blind sides.

Double- and triple-teaming is when two or three blockers are assigned to bring you down instead of the usual one. It is true that when a defensive lineman is double-teamed or triple-teamed, he must be doing something right. Even so, no one enjoys taking on two or three blockers instead of just one, but we must understand that the greater the threat we become to the enemy, the more opposition he will assign to defeat us. As frustrating as this can be, to the lineman or to the Christian, we must understand that this will make it easier for our teammates. Even though the devil may have taken a third of the angels with him, he is still outnumbered two to one! Since demons do not reproduce, there is a limited number of them. The more we keep tied up, the less demonic opposition other Christians will suffer. Except for the egotist, it does not matter who makes the big play. What matters is that our team wins. Even though we may at times get "stopped" by demonic opposition, we may have still served a great purpose by opening the way for someone else to break through. Our goal must always be to play the game with all of our heart, and leave the results to God.

Practice Determines Success

There is much more to being a successful football player than being in shape. Because we are a team we must practice together until we know each other's skills, judgment and even shortcomings as well as we know our own. When a play is called, everyone must know and fulfill their assignment for it to be successful.

The same principles are true for the church, which is called to be the ultimate team. The only difference is that in the church we do not have much time to practice—we are thrust immediately into a life and death struggle of far greater importance than any game. We are fighting for the glory of the Lord and the souls of men! Even so, we must learn to know our teammates, depending on each other's skills and filling in for each other's weaknesses. We must all be using the same "play book," carefully carrying out our own assignments, but in harmony with the rest of the team. The more we work together, the more we learn how we each react in certain circumstances, and the greater the harmony we will have.

There is just no substitute for properly preparing for a game. To do this we work on our conditioning, skills and plays, and we spend a considerable amount of time watching and analyzing film of our opponents. Studying game films can show us offensive alignments where they might run

> *"The greater the threat we become to the enemy, the more opposition he will assign to defeat us."*

a double-team or a "crack-back" block. Sometimes we notice a certain stance the linemen take that might give away what the next play could be.

The Christian's primary "game film" is the Bible. From Genesis through Revelation it describes the tactics of the enemy. Those who are ignorant of the enemy's schemes will often be surprised and blindsided. Those who know the Word of God will seldom be caught off guard by what the enemy does.

> *"Our goal must always be to play the game with all of our heart, and leave the results to God."*

An old proverb says, "Practice makes perfect." That statement is only true if you are practicing what is right. Practicing the wrong fundamentals can actually hinder you. If we practice all week expecting our opposing team to primarily run the ball, and they come out passing, they will probably have us at a disadvantage the whole game.

Our Coach, Jesus, knows the enemy better than the enemy knows himself. We must listen to Him and follow His game plan if we are to be prepared. If we don't, we may be well-prepared for the enemy to come against our physical resources, when his attack comes against our families. We may go into a city with a great evangelistic campaign when the Lord knows that the church in that city needs to be strengthened before it will be able to raise and equip the new believers. When the game starts, it's too late to think about whether you're prepared or not. Your preparation will be glaringly displayed, good or bad, throughout the course of the game. The same will be true of our spiritual preparation. As Paul wrote to Timothy:

Be diligent [train] to present yourself approved to God as a workman who does not need to be ashamed, handling accurately the word of truth (II Timothy 2:15).

In practice we all like to give the most attention to what we do the best. However, to be properly prepared we often need to give more attention to our weaknesses. If we have trouble understanding the Word of God we need to make that a primary devotion in our training. If we are weak in prayer, we need to seek the Lord's help in making that a strength. It is the grace of God to turn our weaknesses into strengths (see II Corinthians 12:9). The rebuke in Hebrews 5:12-14 still applies to much of the church today.

In fact, though by this time you ought to be teachers, you need someone to teach you the elementary truths of God's word all over again. You need milk, not solid food!

Anyone who lives on milk, being still an infant, is not acquainted with the teaching about righteousness.

But solid food is for the mature, who by constant use have trained themselves to distinguish good from evil (NIV).

I really like the way the *Living Bible* paraphrases verse 14:

You will never be able to eat solid spiritual food and understand the deeper things of God's Word until you become better Christians and learn right from wrong by practicing doing right.

In the same way we as Christians must study God's Word, and surround ourselves with other believers who *practice* what is right. A football player knows if he doesn't show his commitment by his actions he will be cut from the team. Likewise, one who may not be as skilled as another will often be kept on the team, as he is a hard worker and good for morale, which means that his attitude inspires others to work hard as well. A player with a bad attitude, even if the most skilled player, can cause the failure of a whole team.

To be on one of God's championship teams that accomplishes something significant, we do not need physical skills, but we do need faith, which will always be revealed by an overcoming attitude. The ten spies who gave a bad report on the Promised Land caused their whole generation to fall short of their potential destiny. Joshua and Caleb, the two spies who had the good report, were used by God to lead the next generation into their inheritance.

Accountability for Victory

Accountability seems to be a forgotten art these days in America. We pride ourselves on our independence. Everybody wants to do his own thing, and nobody wants to answer to anyone else except himself. Can you imagine what a football team would be like if no one was accountable to anyone else? If no one respected the authority of the coach there would be so much argument and debate just deciding on which play to run that it would be impossible to even play a game.

Many churches disqualify themselves from participation in something truly meaningful by such a lack of respect for authority. Accountability is basically responsibility, and responsibility means *the ability to respond.* If we are going to be

effective spiritually we are going to have to develop a character that is contrary to this disruptive spirit of the age.

The best leaders on any team will be those who best follow the coach's directives. The best leaders in Christ are the best followers of Christ; it is those He sends as His representatives. The sports teams that are the most successful are built on a strong foundation of teamwork and accountability. The churches that are the most successful will have done likewise.

The church is called to be a reflection of the wisdom and greatness of the greatest coach, Jesus. He is right now putting together a team that will win it all. Before the end, His team will demonstrate to the world what discipline, teamwork, focused vision, and resolve mean. When we all stand on that great judgment day to watch the "game films" of history, the spiritual "big plays" will be given their place, but I believe that we will also come to fully understand that it was "in the trenches," the daily victories of ordinary believers, which were really responsible for the victory. No one here may notice you, but eternity is watching. Regardless of who you are, and what your position is, your's can be one of the most important parts of all. Discipline yourself to line up and play every day with all of your heart. You're playing in something much bigger than the Superbowl! ■

Reggie White is a defensive lineman for the Green Bay Packers. A future Hall of Famer, he is considered by many to be one of the best defensive players of all time. Reggie is also an ordained Baptist minister and the founder of The National Society of Nehemiah, which is devoted to inner-city ministry. This is a modified article taken from Reggie's book *Minister of Defense*, which can be found in Christian bookstores everywhere, or may be ordered directly from Morning-Star Publications.

CHANGES IN THE WIND

BY BOB SORGE

All Scriptures NKJV unless otherwise noted.

Some portions of the body of Christ are sensing a change in the winds of the Spirit in regard to praise and worship. The Charismatic Renewal witnessed an upsurge in vibrant celebration and worship. In the mid-80s, another wave of worship crested in the church as worship seminars proliferated, books and tapes on worship suddenly abounded, and the explosion of ministries like Integrity's *Hosanna* music caught the attention and appreciation of the international church. And now in the mid-90s, there seems to be another shift in the impetus of the Spirit.

This time the change that seems to be in the air is somewhat difficult to understand and label. We don't understand why, but for some of us, the forms of worship that we've employed for years are becoming less exciting. Something resembling boredom is creeping into our services, and we're realizing that the Holy Spirit is simply not energizing the forms of worship that were incredibly powerful in the Spirit just a few short years ago.

One well-known worship leader told me he foresees a change in our "paradigm of worship." I have observed that ministries which flourished in the "praise and worship movement" are finding it more difficult to balance their budgets. What once seemed fresh and vital has become repetitive and at times contrived. How is the stream changing? Where is the stream taking us?

Recently, the Lord began to unfold some thoughts to my heart that seemed significant to understanding the times we're in. These thoughts are derived from the story of the "Triumphal Entry," when Jesus rode on a donkey into Jerusalem to the boisterous praises of His followers. I invite you to consider these thoughts:

The triumphal entry is an example of corporate worship. This was the first and only time in the earthly life of Jesus that a crowd gathered to praise Him openly and extravagantly. For three years Jesus had been telling His followers, "Don't tell anyone!" But now the Father was giving the green light: "Let them praise You, Son."

Jesus set the stage for this drama of corporate hosannas. He ordered up the donkey and rode upon it, inspiring the prophetic spirit of praise within those of His followers who understood this fulfillment of Scripture (see Matthew 21:2-5; Luke 19:38). In setting things up like this, and also by doing nothing to stop the praising crowds, we can easily say that Jesus was encouraging and aiding their praises. Something in His demeanor evoked pleasure in and approval of their praises, which only fueled the crowd's enthusiasm. And when His critics asked Him to rebuke the praisers, He made one of the greatest pronouncements ever on praise: **"I tell you that if these should keep silent, the stones would immediately cry out" (Luke 19:40).** Three years of wonder at the works of God were pent up in these people (see Luke 19:37), and when they realized Jesus was supportive, they literally burst forth with loud and high acclamations.

The praises of the people were audible, enthusiastic, uninhibited and highly expressive. Their praise was not only spoken, but also expressed very dramatically and visually in the way they spread a carpet of clothing and branches for the King's colt to walk upon (see Matthew 21:7-8).

I see a similarity between this point in the triumphal entry, and where we've been in the body of Christ in recent years. The Lord has been calling the church to extroverted, uninhibited, expressive worship. He has been equipping His worshipers with practical tools and how-to's for implementing expressive worship in local churches. There have been equipping seminars, books, tapes, etc., to teach peo-

"We've learned the art of high praise under the smile of Jesus, and now we're sensing a change in the atmosphere, but we're still trying to keep the people up in high praises."

ple how to express themselves freely in the presence of God. We've seen the pleasure in the face of Christ as we've prepared a path of praise for the King.

But in the story of the triumphal entry, a change took place in the atmosphere of the procession, and it happened in Jesus Himself. As He approached the city, His smile gave way to tears, and He began to weep over the city (see Luke 19:41). "Jesus, you're throwing a damper on the meeting. We're having the praise party of the decade, and You're getting all sorrowful. We're doing our best to keep the crowd up, but we need you to cooperate with the effort, Lord." They didn't understand the shift that was taking place in the Spirit.

We're in a similar place in the mid-90s. We've learned the art of high praise under the smile of Jesus, and now we're sensing a change in the atmosphere, but we're still trying to keep the people up in high praises. We don't understand what's changing, but the expression on Jesus' countenance is different.

The thing that removed Jesus' smile at the triumphal entry was the flood of emotions that swept over His soul as He realized He was coming to Jerusalem as the Lamb, to be slain by the people to whom He had come. His eyes turned to Calvary, and they flowed with tears as He considered the judgment that would come upon the resistant nation of Israel. The "praise party" was an important preparatory element in the unfolding events of that final week, but the heart of Jesus began to be broken for those who were rejecting Him.

Because of the diversity in the body of Christ, different segments of the church are at different places at different times. If you're in a place in any way similar to where I am at, you can probably agree that Jesus' countenance has changed, and even though we're maintaining the praise forms we've become comfortable with, we realize that something has changed. We don't sense the smile of Jesus on what we're doing like we used to. And like the disciples of 2,000 years ago, we're looking at this new face of Jesus, and we don't know what to do in response.

"Whatever our response needs to be, I believe it will include an embracing of the cross and a passion for the harvest. Jesus at one time was calling us to rejoice, but now He's calling us to die."

Whatever our response needs to be, I believe it will include an embracing of the cross and a passion for the harvest. Jesus at one time was calling us to rejoice, but now He's calling us to die. The age of the Old Covenant was consummated with the death of Jesus on the cross; in the same way, the age of the New Covenant will come into full consummation when the people of God embrace the fullness of the cross. The Spirit is kindling a passion for Jesus in the hearts of His people, and the best way to be renewed in love is to have a revelation of the love of God displayed in the cross of Jesus Christ.

One of the "paradigm shifts" currently taking place in the body of Christ, in my opinion, is a moving away from an emphasis on the mechanics of worship (the how-to's), and a renewed emphasis on the Person Whom we worship. There is a cry in our hearts to know Jesus Himself, in the fullness of His personality— to have mature bridal affection for our Lord. Some of us have been more enthralled with the praise party than with the King. But our hearts are burning and being quickened, for we are coming alive to the infinitely glorious personality of our Lover and Friend. This is not just spirited worship, but worship in truth—an unfolding understanding of Who Jesus really is.

We must know how the heart of Jesus is changing as we journey toward the culmination of all things. To do this we must be searching His face. Just a little while ago He was laughing, but what's He doing now? When we see the weeping Savior, will we know how to respond? ∎

Bob Sorge is pastor of Zion Fellowship in Canandaigua, NY. He served for three years as Director of Music at Elim Bible Institute, Lima, NY where he established a training program for worship leaders. Author of the widely acclaimed book, *Exploring Worship*, Bob has just written another book, *In His Face: A Prophetic Call to Renewed Focus* (available through Christian bookstores). Bob and his wife, Marci, enjoy serving the Lord in Canandaigua, where they reside with their three children.

Mustard Seeds of Wisdom

"I used to preach that God was behind the sinner with a double-edged sword, ready to hew him down. I have got done with that. I preach now that God is behind the sinner with love, and he is running away from the God of love."

— *Dwight L. Moody*

CULTIVATING SPIRITUAL HUNGER

BY WADE TAYLOR

TEACHING

All Scriptures KJV unless otherwise noted.

Draw me, we will run after thee: the king hath brought me into his chambers (Song of Solomon 1:4).

The Song of Solomon is a beautiful portrayal of the relationship between a bridegroom and his bride. Not only is it a prophetic picture of Christ's relationship with the church, it also holds significant insights for each believer who desires a deeper intimacy with our Lord.

The first part of this verse expresses a prayer that is vital to our spiritual health and well being; **"Draw me."** It uses only two words so it may easily be remembered and prayed often. Next, follows a commitment telling the Lord that we will follow Him, if He will answer the first part of our prayer and create within us a spiritual hunger; **"We will run after thee."** The third part is the marvelous result of the outworking of the first two; **"The king hath brought me into his chambers."**

This extremely important prayer, **"Draw me,"** relates to the hunger drive that is resident within each one of us in varied degrees, which is at the foundation of all life. This drive, a fundamental urge of all life, seeks its satisfaction in many ways. Our spiritual hunger is a part of this.

A baby is born hungry. The mother cannot create this hunger; she can only feed it. The spiritual hunger that is within us is a creative act of God and comes only from Him. It cannot be created or imparted by man. We must look to the Lord alone for this. He will create and then enlarge our spiritual hunger as we ask Him to cause us to become spiritually hungry. Then through His Word, through fellowship with Him, and through anointed ministry, He will feed and satisfy this hunger.

This enlargement of our spiritual capacity takes place as we hold ourselves before the Lord and actively "wait upon Him." When it comes, we must be careful to separate this newly enlarged spiritual desire from other desires and not allow some substitute to seemingly satisfy it. Nor should we seek some other means than the Lord Himself to satisfy our spiritual hunger.

As this hunger within us becomes more intense and we cry out for satisfaction, the Lord will respond and, as we "feed Him"

26 THE MORNING STAR

with our commitment to "run after Him," He in turn will "feed us." He is a seeking God who is very anxious for our fellowship.

> **Behold, I stand at the door, and knock: if any man hear my voice, and open the door, I will come in to him, and will sup with him [we feed Him], and He with me [He feeds us] (Revelation 3:20).**

As this spiritual hunger provokes us to "open the door" to a relationship of intimate personal communion with our Lord, it will result in our growing spiritually. Spiritual hunger is the foundation of our spiritual life and of our growth into spiritual maturity.

The next step is our commitment, **"We will run after thee."** "We" speaks of every part of our being totally seeking after and responding to the Lord. Paul said, **"I am crucified with Christ: nevertheless I live; yet not I, but Christ liveth in me" (Galatians 2:20).** We may memorize this verse, quote it, and even testify about it, but there is a principle that must be applied; Truth is never ours until we have experienced it. When the result of our experience has been made real within us, only then will it become a part of us.

The Lord will respond to this commitment, **"we will run,"** and will cause His Word to become an experiential reality within our life. He will accomplish this by arranging all of the necessary circumstances within our daily pattern of life to bring about this personal, experiential understanding of the written Word. Scripture tells us concerning Jesus, **"The Word was made flesh, and dwelt among us" (John 1:14).** Only as the Word of God becomes a personalized reality within our life experience will we be able to witness to its truth and power.

"Truth is never ours until we have experienced it. When the result of our experience has been made real within us, only then will it become a part of us."

When Jesus was baptized by John, the heavens opened as He came up out of the waters. The Spirit of God descended as a dove and settled upon Him as the Father said, **"This is my beloved Son, in whom I am well pleased" (Matthew 3:17).** This was a tremendous blessing, but there was something more that Jesus needed to experience before this word that He received from His Father could become "flesh" (an experiential reality) in His life. We see this after Jesus came up out of the water full of the Holy Ghost.

> **And Jesus being full of the Holy Ghost returned from Jordan, and was led by the Spirit into the wilderness,**
> **Being forty days tempted of the devil (Luke 4:1-2).**

He had received the blessing and the impartation. Now, the Word that had been spoken over Him was to be personalized, or made "flesh" within His life experience. The next thing the Scripture tells us is that "He was driven." Jesus was compelled by the Holy Spirit to go into the wilderness (see Mark 1:12). There, He was tested for forty days; forty being the number of testing. By the end of this time, He had overcome every temptation, and had totally defeated Satan.

Jesus then came forth from the wilderness in the power of the Spirit.

And Jesus returned in the power of the Spirit into Galilee: and there went out a fame of him through all the region round about (Luke 4:14).

The *fullness* had become *power* because truth had been personalized in His life through experience. The Scripture tells us that **"we are his workmanship" (Ephesians 2:10),** and that He is working in our lives, not just to get us to heaven, but rather to conform us to the image and likeness of Jesus Christ (see Romans 8:29). At this present time, the Lord is bringing forth those who are willing to be tested and proven that they might be able to buy of Him **"gold tried in the fire."**

I counsel thee to buy of me gold tried in the fire, that thou mayest be rich; and white raiment, that thou mayest be clothed, and that the shame of thy nakedness do not appear; and anoint thine eyes with eyesalve, that thou mayest see (Revelation 3:18).

The Lord is seeking a people who are not spiritually lazy, or content to rest in the fullness of the Spirit that they have received, but who are pressing onward until they have experienced the *power* of the Spirit. There are those who are willing to wait in the wilderness and suffer intense hunger, until they have been fed by the Lord Himself. These will come forth victorious in the power of the Spirit. Indeed the world desperately needs such in this day.

Acts 1:8 tells us, **"But ye shall receive power, *after*."** Power in our Christian experience does not come as a result of our receiving the fullness of the Spirit. There is something more required for His power to come into our lives.

Jesus received the fullness of the Spirit in the Jordan, but went into the wilderness for a time of testing and proving. Here, the Word became flesh, or power in His life. Now, when Jesus ministered, men became attentive and said, **"Never man spake like this man" (John 7:46).** Why? Because the Word and the flesh (His life experience) had become one. This is the oneness which the Lord desires to work into our lives.

If we are sincere in praying, **"draw me,"** and then make this unconditional consecration to the Lord, **"we will run after thee,"** the Lord will begin the process of leading us to Himself. While in the time of our wilderness testing, the Lord will give us the baptism in the Holy Spirit, the gifts and the blessings that follow, along with all the experiences that are necessary to bring us into the experiential knowledge of His power. As we faithfully pass through these experiences, His Word and His presence will become more than just a blessing or testimony. It will become spiritual power, personalized in our life, bringing us into a unity of purpose and oneness with the Lord.

And they were astonished at his doctrine: for his word was with power (Luke 4:32).

"We will run after thee." *"Lord, we—the total me: spirit, soul and body; my will, my intellect, and my emotions, all that I*

"While in the time of our wilderness testing, the Lord will give us the baptism in the Holy Spirit, the gifts and the blessings that follow, along with all the experiences that are necessary to bring us into the experiential knowledge of His power."

ever was, all that I am now, and all that I ever will be—all of me; we will respond to Your hand upon my life and Your activity within me. The Word that You quickened to me, the revelation that You showed to me, all that You have given to me must be incorporated into my life experience, in union with You. Lord, come, and I will lovingly and submissively respond to You, as You accomplish all this within me."

The Scripture tells us, **"many are called, but few are chosen" (Matthew 22:14).** Another way to say this is: "Many are called, but few are willing to pay the price in order to be chosen." There is a price to pay in coming into the place where His Word has been personalized in our life experience. Then, when we speak, we bear witness to this impartation of His Word becoming flesh in our lives. Now, "His Word and my life" have become one, and "we" in this oneness will run after Him.

> **But ye shall receive power, after that the Holy Ghost is come upon you:** *and ye shall be witnesses unto me* **(Acts 1:8).**

There is a popular saying that the baptism in the Holy Spirit is "power for service." This is true, but this baptism is much more than that. This power that we receive is the *dunamis* (Greek for "dynamo") of God; it is the enabling power of God that flows into our lives. It enables and guides us into our identification with Him.

When Moses went up into the Mount, the children of Israel said to him, **"All that the LORD hath spoken we will do" (Exodus 19:8).** This was a tremendous statement, but they failed. The Old Testament is

"There is a price to pay in coming into the place where His Word has been personalized in our life experience."

written as a testimony that flesh cannot fulfill the law of God. Flesh cannot, but the promise of a New Covenant was given in which the Lord said,

> **A new heart also will I give you, and a new spirit will I put within you: and I will take away the stony heart out of your flesh, and I will give you an heart of flesh.**
>
> **And I will put my spirit within you, and cause you to walk in my statutes, and ye shall keep my judgments and do them (Ezekiel 36:26-27).**

The baptism in the Holy Spirit is given as the fulfillment of these verses. It is the power of the Holy Spirit which will cause, or enable us to walk in His statutes. The "power" in Acts 1:8 is the same as the "cause" in Ezekiel 36:27. These are one and the same. Thus, the baptism in the Holy Spirit is far more than power for service. Christian service is something that we "do" for the Lord. However, this verse does not say anything about doing; rather, it tells us that we are to "be" a witness.

"Being" speaks of what I am, rather than what I "do." It is the expression of what I have become in Him. If I am "doing" witnessing, then I am telling someone about the Lord. However, if I am "being" a witness, there is something far deeper. In "being" a witness, I am saying or doing exactly what Jesus would do or say if He were here. Therefore, I am a "witness" or a "sample" of Him. The baptism will truly enable us to serve Him better, but the real result is that through the power that is imparted into our lives, we become a witness that can be seen as well as heard.

That which I have experienced and become is reflected through my conduct. Now, my life will be a witness of these things. When Philip said, **"Show us the Father"** (John 14:8). Jesus' reply was, **"He that hath seen me hath seen the Father"** (verse 9). Jesus was saying, "My life is a witness of the Father to such an extent that if you have seen Me, you have seen the Father."

His processings begin in our lives only after it is proven to the Lord that we truly meant it when we told Him we would run after Him. **"Ye shall receive power, *after*."** The baptism in the Holy Spirit is a gift. But, the power is only available to us "after." We must go through a time of testing in order to come into the experience of this power.

We asked the Lord to **"draw us."** Then, we consecrated our lives to **"run after thee."** However, there is another step that we are to take. **"The king hath brought me into his chambers"** (Song of Solomon 1:4). Here, as we come into the intimacy of His manifest presence, we will receive the enabling power that will guide us through the steps that will lead us into spiritual maturity. Now, we will be able to enjoy increasing communion and fellowship with Him.

In order to gain the capacity and strength for these times of testing, He brings us into His chambers, where we spend time with Him in the intimacy of His manifest presence. Here, we wait before Him and bask in His presence. This time that we spend waiting on the Lord is of the utmost importance.

But they that wait upon the LORD shall renew their strength; they shall mount up with wings as eagles; they shall run, and not be weary; and they shall walk, and not faint (Isaiah 40:31).

"The King hath brought me into His chambers." Herein is the secret: We *must* spend time in communion with the Lord. When we come into His chambers, and wait in His presence, the power of God flows into our being. Then, we are enabled to minister, witness, or move in what we have received. Our strength will run down, but **"they that wait upon the LORD shall renew their strength."** Now, we will daily have the strength to face the testings and problems of life.

Our Heavenly Bridegroom brings us into His chambers to abide there with Him. As His Bride, we will experience joy unspeakable, unknown to others. During these times of intimate communion with Him, we are brought closer to being made one with Him, and increasingly we understand spiritual principles and truths.

As we pray this little prayer, **"Draw me,"** we are opening the way that leads us into the chambers of heaven. There, all that we long for is found in Him. **"The king hath brought me into his chambers."** ■

Wade Taylor is the founder and director of Pinecrest Bible Training Center in Salisbury Center, New York. Wade is known for his deep and sincere passion for Jesus. This article is an excerpt from his book, *The Secret of the Stairs*, which is an exposition of the Song of Solomon. It can be ordered by sending $6.95, plus $1.75 S/H, to Wade Taylor, c/o Pinecrest BTC, PO Box 320, Salisbury Center, NY 13454-0320.

THE REWARDS OF ALMSGIVING

BY DAVID ALSOBROOK

All Scriptures NAS unless otherwise noted.

Beware of practicing your righteousness before men to be noticed by them; otherwise you have no reward with your Father who is in heaven.

When therefore you give alms, do not sound a trumpet before you, as the hypocrites do in the synagogues and in the streets, that they may be honored by men. Truly I say to you, they have their reward in full.

But when you give alms, do not let your left hand know what your right hand is doing

that your alms may be in secret; and your Father who sees in secret will repay you (Matthew 6:1-4).

Almsgiving was widely practiced in ancient Israel and the early church, but we don't hear a great deal about it today. *Almsgiving is the practice of benevolence, a charitable deed on behalf of a needy person.* Alms can be given in the form of cash, food, or other commodities. Even time and service given to aid someone in need are viewed as alms—such as helping a stranded motorist, etc. Widows, orphans, and the disabled are presented as especially worthy recipients of alms in the Scriptures.

In the Old Testament, the word *tsedaqah* is translated "righteousness" in our English versions. It is interesting that this word is also used for "almsdeeds," since there is no precise word for "alms" in the Hebrew language. According to *Unger's Bible Dictionary*, righteousness and almsgiving eventually became interchangeable in Hebrew thought. In fact, almsdeeds are thought to be the meaning of "righteousness" in these specific passages:

Treasurers of wickedness profit nothing, but righteousness [almsgiving] delivers from death (Proverbs 10:2 NKJV).

Riches do not profit in the day of wrath, but righteousness [almsgiving] delivers from death (Proverbs 11:4 NKJV).

Notice that Jesus began His teaching on almsgiving with the phrase, *"Beware of practicing your righteousness before men"* (Matthew 6:1), thus equating righteousness with almsgiving. One of the most righteous things a person can do is to give alms. James expressed it this way:

External religious worship [religion as it is expressed in outward acts] that is pure and unblemished in the sight of God the Father is this: to visit and help and care for the orphans and widows in their affliction and need, and to keep oneself unspotted and uncontaminated from the world (James 1:27 AMP).

Three Areas of Giving

Every Christian should tithe, offer, and give alms. If any of these three areas is lacking, so will our spiritual life be lacking. Alms are often confused with tithes and offerings. Tithing is the practice of returning a tenth of one's income to the Lord, usually at one's home church. An offering is a financial gift over and above the tithe, of any amount the Lord lays on the offerer's heart. Offerings can be given to the Lord through either the local church or through outreach ministries. (Churches depend on tithes as their primary support base; outreach ministries are entirely supported by offerings.)

Unlike either tithes or offerings, alms are given directly to the needy person and ideally should be unknown to any but the giver and recipient. (It's most desirable that the recipient not know his benefactor, but this is not always possible.)

But when you give alms, do not let your left hand know what your hand is doing that your alms may be in secret; and your Father who sees in secret will repay you (Matthew 6:3-4).

"Every Christian should tithe, offer, and give alms. If any of these three areas is lacking, so will our spiritual life be lacking."

Sadly, only a small percentage of the Lord's people regularly tithe. Even fewer give offerings above the tithe. Only a tiny fraction of God's people give alms. Please keep in mind some important distinctives about these three different types of giving:

Tithing is a tenth given to the local church,

Offerings are above the tithe and can be given to outreach ministries,

Alms are given directly to the needy. By their nature, alms are private and personal. Alms are the essence of charity—giving without thought of return or personal gain. Alms should be performed in Jesus' name resulting in His glory.

The privacy surrounding alms does not apply to tithes and offerings. Jesus Himself sat over the treasury as the people brought their tithes and offerings to the Lord during public temple worship (see Mark 12:41-44). When we tithe and offer to the Lord it is not required that we shroud these types of giving in secrecy, although we would never want to make a show of any part of our giving.

Some believers, mistaking alms for tithes and offerings, will not write checks or fill out offering envelopes. They place their tithes and offerings in unmarked envelopes and have someone else drop it in the collection plate for them. It is not wrong to write checks, beloved, or accept tax receipts for tithes and offerings. Sometimes in giving alms we have to do it in a less than secret manner—although secrecy should always be our goal—but if our heart is right, our almsgift is surely pleasing to the Lord. Christ's main concern focused on the proper way to give alms: **"Take heed** that ye do not your righteousness before men, *to be seen of them*" (Matthew 6:1 ASV).

There is something about human nature that wants to be recognized for benevolent service (Have you ever watched a telethon?). Jesus taught that it is wrong to perform good deeds in anticipation of men's praise. Rather, we are to look for our Father's smile of approval and await His reward for our private deeds of charity. Otherwise, the deed itself may have been beneficial to the needy, but we will not be rewarded by our Heavenly Father. Notice that Jesus did not say, "But *if* you give alms." He said, **"But *when* you give alms"** because He expected it to be a regular part of Christian lifestyle.

The religious leaders of that time sounded loud trumpets when assisting any beggar who sat along the roadside. Jesus condemned their hypocritical parade, assuring them that the only reward they had for their benevolence was already paid in full through the beggar's thanks. The attitude of our hearts is the obvious point: *motives must be scrutinized.* Today, we should ask ourselves "Am I giving to be seen or thanked by men or is my motive purely to help this needy one and glorify God?"

When our motivation is pure there is great reward laid up in heaven for our acts of benevolence. Temporal gifts can result in eternal treasures. As Jesus concluded His teaching on almsgiving, prayer, and fasting He said,

So that you may not be seen fasting by men, but by your Father who is in secret; and your Father who sees in secret will repay you.

Do not lay up for yourselves treasures upon earth, where moth and rust destroy, and where thieves break in and steal.

But lay up for yourselves treasures in heaven, **where neither moth nor rust destroys, and where thieves do not break in or steal (Matthew 6:18-20).**

It is obvious, interpreting it in the context, that the primary way we lay up heavenly treasures is by giving alms, praying, and fasting in the proper ways. Heavenly treasures also result in immediate blessings as well as eternal ones.

> *"It is obvious, interpreting it in the context, that the primary way we lay up heavenly treasures is by giving alms, praying, and fasting in the proper ways."*

Except when given through a charitable organization, or relief fund specifically designated for the needy, alms are to be as private as possible. It is not always practical to give alms privately, however, and the early church sometimes received public collections for the poor (see Acts 11:29-30; I Corinthians 16:1). One type of almsgiving for those of us living in North America, the support of orphans, almost always has to be done through charitable organizations, since most uncared-for orphans live in Third World countries where we ourselves cannot go. There are several reputable organizations that give you the name, age, photograph, and other pertinent information about the child you sponsor. This makes it exciting as we can pray for and develop a personal correspondence with the child as he or she grows.

When alms cannot be given secretly or anonymously, we must carefully direct the recipient's appreciation to the Lord and not to ourselves, for if He had not moved upon our heart we surely would have not remembered the poor. Since many recipients are not born-again, they are likely to express gratitude to the channel of God's blessing, rather than to God Himself. This is why great effort should be made to obey Paul's admonition in all our good deeds: **"And whatever you do in word or deed, do all in the name of the Lord Jesus, giving thanks through Him to God the Father" (Colossians 3:17).** Always direct a person's attention to the Lord, no matter what you are doing.

Proper almsgiving ascends before the throne of God and brings heaven's smile like nothing else! Consider these Scriptures:

> **And Cornelius said, "Four days ago to this hour, I was praying in my house during the ninth hour; and behold, a man stood before me in shining garments,**
>
> **and he said, 'Cornelius, your prayer has been heard and *your alms have been remembered before God'* " (Acts 10:30-31).**
>
> **He who despises his neighbor sins, but *happy is he who is gracious to the poor* (Proverbs 14:21).**
>
> **He who is gracious to a poor man lends to the LORD, and *He will repay him for his good deed* (Proverbs 19:17).**
>
> **Therefore, O king, may my advice be pleasing to you: *break away* now from your sins by doing righteousness, and *from your iniquities by showing mercy to the poor*, in case there may be a prolonging of your prosperity (Daniel 4:27).**

Jesus Practiced Almsgiving

Almsgiving in ancient Israel, as I said earlier, was widely practiced. Jesus did not have to instruct His hearers, therefore, on the importance of giving alms, since conscientious Jews regularly practiced benevolence.

Jesus, of course, habitually practiced almsgiving. His instruction to Judas during the Last Supper (**"What you do, do quickly"**) was interpreted by some at the table to mean that Jesus' treasurer was to go, at once, and dispense aid to the poor. They were evidently accustomed to their Master's frequent benevolence, so they paid little attention as Judas went "out into the night" of eternal darkness on his mission of betrayal (see John 13:27-30).

Jesus demonstrated His care for the poor numerous times. He instructed the rich, young ruler to sell everything he had and give it to the poor (see Matthew 19:21; Luke 18:22). He authenticated His ministry to John's disciples, in part, by informing them that the gospel was being preached to the poor, just as He had announced this as His first objective when He commenced His ministry (see Matthew 11:5; Luke 4:18). Christ said we would always have the poor among us and whenever we so desire we may benefit them (see Matthew 26:11).

The Example of the Early Church

The early disciples did not forget this important practice. When James, John and Peter, pillars of the Jerusalem church, examined Paul's doctrine and ministry they extended the right hand of fellowship to him, exhorting him in only one area:

> **They only [made one stipulation], that we were to remember the poor,**

which very thing I was also eager to do (Galatians 2:10 AMP).

As I pondered this verse my heart was struck by the phrase **"remember the poor."** It's easy to forget them. With our busy schedules and family demands, the homeless and needy don't come easily to our minds. With our own bills and financial obligations, it is easy to push almsgiving to the bottom of the list. I was also impressed by the importance the Jerusalem Pillars placed on ministries supporting the poor! Their unselfishness is a character trait all church leaders should follow.

In my study of this subject I found it amazing that one of the most popular sayings of Jesus, **"It is more blessed to give than to receive,"** was actually spoken in the context of almsgiving:

> **In everything I have pointed out to you [by example] that, by working diligently thus *we ought to assist the weak*, being mindful of the words of the Lord Jesus, how He Himself said, It is more blessed—makes one happier and more to be envied—to give than to receive (Acts 20:35 AMP).**

Paul, in this verse, was preparing to leave, never to return to Ephesus. In his emotionally-charged farewell, the apostle warned the saints of various errors which they were to guard against. On the positive side he exhorted them to assist the weak (care for the poor) as he had shown them by his example. Paul undergirded his admonition by quoting a popular saying of Jesus which is not found in any of the Gospels, but which was widely circulated among the early Christians: "It is more blessed to give than to receive." The popularity of this saying continues to the present, probably due to the striking paradox

it presents to our basic fallen nature. Is it not true that even Christians think more about how happy it would make us to receive an unexpected financial blessing than we think about how happy we would be to give unto others? Jesus said it actually makes one happier to give an unexpected financial gift than it does to receive such a gift, and this goes against the grain of natural thinking.

I can personally witness to the truth of the Lord's statement. There have been countless times during the past two decades of ministry when I was pressed financially and suddenly received an unexpected gift which greatly lifted my load. The joy at receiving such a blessing was considerable, as you can imagine, and the thanksgiving in my heart flowed freely, *but the joy of receiving pales beside the joy of giving!*

Chain-Reaction Blessings

Almsgiving can result in "chain-reaction blessings." A true story best illustrates what I mean by this term. I rarely tell anyone about any personal alms I give because, as we have seen, Jesus exhorted us to secrecy in almsgiving. As I was working on this article I sensed the Holy Spirit urging me to share with you, for your encouragement, one particular example of almsgiving.

Back in 1985 I was sending my book on abortion to every church in America—no small task for a ministry the size of ours! I was in prayer one morning asking the Lord to send in tens of thousands of dollars when the Holy Spirit impressed the amount of $79 on my heart for a dear widow friend whom I will call "Nancy."

Nancy's husband had been taken years before and had not left her much in the way of insurance or provision. She was left with two sons to raise and very little money.

Nancy was quite successful in this endeavor as both sons are solid Christian husbands today (one is even a minister).

I was blessed when God spoke this exact amount to my heart because I knew the Living God was in direct communion with me, not only speaking to me, but hearing my request as well. I finished praying and answered mail for a few hours. Suddenly, I sensed it was time to carry out the Lord's instruction. I did not want Nancy to be home when I came by, in keeping with Christ's command that the left hand not know what the right hand is doing, so I dialed her number to see whether or not she was home. (If she was home I was just going to talk with her in a general way and not tell her I had a gift.) My phone call went unanswered, so I knew she was probably gone. I placed four twenties in a plain envelope and headed for her house, which was only eight or nine miles away.

As I was driving a little Voice said, "Did I say *$80?*" So, I stopped at a convenience store and broke a twenty. When I arrived at her house I hurriedly placed the unmarked envelope between the screen door and front door and left. I drove back to my office with a sense of deep peace and forgot all about it.

A couple of days later I was attending the mid-week service at our home church when Nancy stood up and requested permission to share a testimony. Our pastor nodded his approval. Nancy laughed and cried as she told everyone how her old car had been needing repairs for some time, so she had taken it in to the garage for service. A Christian mechanic, who knew of her

"Is it not true that even Christians think more about how happy it would make us to receive an unexpected financial blessing than we think about how happy we would be to give unto others?"

fixed income, had given her a generous "parts only, no labor" estimate, but had called her with the sad news midway through the job that the vehicle needed more repairs. He reluctantly told her he had been forced to spend *$79 more* on parts!

When Nancy hung up the phone she decided to take a walk to a nearby park and have a talk with the Lord. She received the assurance during prayer that her need was met. Unabated joy flooded her soul. She told everyone in that church service that as she came back home her heart could only sing of the goodness of the Lord.

When Nancy opened her front screen door, out fell the envelope. As she reached down she heard herself say aloud, "Here's my $79!" She told us that she was not surprised when she counted out the exact amount on the kitchen table, not one dollar more or less.

Nancy called the mechanic at once and told him how she had just received the $79 he had requested earlier that morning. She told us that this brother in Christ began to praise God loudly as she related her blessing. Immediately spontaneous praise broke out in the church service also. The pastor was led by the Spirit to take prayer requests from the others present and asked Nancy to lead us in prayer. It was a great time! God was glorified! Her testimony caused a chain-reaction of blessings as everyone called out to our gracious God for their needs. A precious liberty was released in the Spirit, and everyone was touched by the goodness of God.

THE REWARDS OF ALMSGIVING

As I witnessed the chain-reaction blessings coming upon that service, I sat in complete, stunned amazement at how God used my small, anonymous gift to bless so many. I remembered how Jesus said, **"Let your light shine before men in such a way that they may see your good works, and glorify your Father who is in heaven"** **(Matthew 5:16).** As Nancy told us, "It is not that $79 was such a big need, but that the need was exactly met at the exact time I needed it. How? Only God knows." God and myself, of course, sitting there drinking it all in, grinning like the cat that swallowed the canary!

By the way, Nancy came to me after the service and exhorted me to trust God for the large financial need she knew I was facing in my ministry at the time. "David, I just read your newsletter and want to encourage you that if God did it for me, He can do it for you. Your needs may be bigger, but they are no more a problem for God than mine was." I looked in the eyes of this dear, older saint and saw such confidence, boldness and assurance in her gaze! My flesh wanted to tell her about my role in her blessing because part of me still wants recognition, but God gave me extra grace so that no one but the Lord was magnified. I looked into those excited eyes and said, "Thank you. I receive your exhortation. Take my hand and agree with me for every cent I need." Nancy did so and within a few weeks every bill was paid and 342,000 churches were mailed a copy of *The Bible Truth on Abortion*, from which thousands of pastors preached to millions of people all across our great land. God is real, after all, isn't He friends? And almsgiving is one of the surest ways to release His blessings!

Most of the time I do not receive specific amounts during prayer, just a general nudge of what I'm to do. I've learned to help the homeless or transients using wisdom, although it takes more effort. Instead of giving them money, I go and purchase what they request and bring it back to them. In so doing, I do not take the risk that my gift will be misused (some who request aid are unscrupulous, but many are sincere). As I hand it to them I always say something like, "I give this to you in the name of the Lord. He loves you and wants to help you with all your problems."

When Was the Last Time You Gave an Almsgift?

Make this a matter of prayer and let God lead you. May you experience the many rewards of almsgiving!

Then the King will say to those on His right, "Come, you who are blessed of My Father, inherit the kingdom prepared for you from the foundation of the world.

For I was hungry, and you gave Me something to eat; I was thirsty, and you gave Me drink; I was a stranger, and you invited Me in;

naked, and you clothed Me; I was sick, and you visited Me; I was in prison, and you came to Me" **(Matthew 25:34-36).** ∎

David Alsobrook has been in full-time evangelistic/teaching ministry most of his life. David and his wife, Dianne, make their home in Nashville, Tennessee, and are the proud parents of three beautiful children. He has written 30 books which have been translated into several languages. David's most recent book, *Learning to Love*, covers the many sides of God's love in everyday life. It is available from Sure Word Ministries, P. O. Box 2305, Brentwood, TN 37024, Phone: (615) 371-1052.

THE MORNING STAR 37

AFTER THE LAUGHTER

BY RICK JOYNER

All Scriptures NAS unless otherwise noted.

Today the church is experiencing a very significant renewal. Churches by the thousands are now experiencing a special touch from God. It is not limited to a single country, denomination, or movement. At the time of this writing it is still growing and spreading at an extraordinary rate.

This movement has so far been characterized mostly by its unique manifestations, such as "holy laughter." There are other manifestations associated with this movement, such as being "slain in the spirit," "quaking" or "jerking," but also others which are disconcerting even to the leaders of the movement. These have been referred to as animal sounds such as "roaring like a lion," and animal actions such as the "duck walk," the "chicken peck," and what appears to be people "soaring like eagles" and "galloping like horses." Is all of this apparent foolishness from the Holy Spirit? Certainly not! However, some of it is, and it is important.

When some of these same manifestations first started breaking out in our meetings, I felt the same kind of atmosphere that

is created when I play with my kids by chasing and tickling them. The longer I play with them the wilder they become. Some of their "manifestations" seemed just like those going on in the meetings. The manifestations were not me, but they were the result of what I was doing to them. Many of the manifestations going on in the meetings are not the Lord, but they are the result of people being touched by Him. They may get a little out of control at times, just as my kids do, but this is much better than the human control which much of the church is still under.

I have been more concerned by some of the theology and attempts to put prophetic significance on these manifestations than I have the manifestations themselves. The last thing I want my kids doing after one of our play sessions is to leave it trying to figure out what this or that kind of tickling meant. The deepest meaning to anything I did was that I just wanted to have fun with them, and I wanted them to enjoy it as much as I did. This is exactly what the Father is doing with His kids in many of these meetings. There is no deep meaning to most of it. To attribute such interpretations is missing the main point. The church is generally sick of empty theology, and simply, desperately desires a touch from God.

In general, the church needs to "lighten up" and learn to just enjoy the Lord sometimes. As Deuteronomy 28:47-48 states, **"Because you did not serve the LORD your God with joy and a glad heart, for the abundance of all things; therefore you shall serve your enemies."** When we lose the joy of the Lord we will go into bondage. There is a time for deeper teachings, for battles, and for weeping, but right now the church is in greater need of this refreshing move that is now sweeping the church. It may have no deeper meaning than that God both loves and enjoys His kids. We must become like children again if we are going to enter His kingdom, and most of us long ago forgot what that means. Something does not have to be deep to be very important.

Chaos versus Order

We must also acknowledge that there are manifestations that are not the result of the Holy Spirit moving on people. God is not the author of confusion, but sometimes man's definition of confusion is confused. When we build something, we like straight lines and everything neatly in place. Have you ever noticed the way the Lord builds a forest? There are no straight lines in a forest. The trees are not neatly in rows, and many are scattered about on the ground in apparent chaos. However, there is an order and harmony in the life cycles of a forest that still defy human comprehension. To be perceived, these cycles must be viewed over a long period of time.

Viewed from our limited perspective, the church also appears to be in chaos. However, from the perspective of the entire church age there is a most extraordinary harmony and purpose that has been unfolding.

When men build a church it will be neat and every line will tend to be straight. When God builds a church it will appear to the natural mind to be chaos. To the one who sees from the perspective of eternity, it will appear in more harmony than any human mind could have conceived. God is a God of order, but to see His order we must be delivered from our natural mind and human perspective.

Even so, it must be acknowledged that there are fleshly manifestations in the present move of God, mostly through weak or insecure people. Other manifestations are demonic. However, it is a mistake to be overly concerned by either of these, as they will always attach themselves to a move of God. The Lord Himself said that every time He sows wheat in a field that the enemy will come along and sow tares "in the same field" (see Matthew 13:24-30). By the standards set by the Lord's own meetings, manifestations in this move of God are still pretty mild.

One of the greatest mistakes that can be made is to try to root out the tares prematurely. The Lord's wisdom was to "let them grow up together" with the wheat, knowing that at the harvest they will be separated. We must understand that it is always part of God's curriculum for His children to grow up with tares in their midst. He even chose Judas for His own inner circle. It may be neater, or more enjoyable if we could get rid of the tares, but those things are obviously not the Lord's highest purpose for any movement.

As a student of church history, especially revivals and reform movements, it does seem that movements that have ultimately gone on to produce the greatest evangelists and reforms of society have had the wildest beginnings. Also, when we look back at history many events seem to have taken place all at once, though they usually unfolded over many years. In each of the Great Awakenings that swept America and Europe, the many salvations, social impact, and heart of the message actually took decades to unfold.

Jonathan Edwards is today regarded as one of the greatest theologians of all time. He is also believed to be one of the greatest intellects ever produced by America. The fruit of the Great Awakening that was sparked by his preaching can still be seen in the basic fabric of both American society and government. It is noteworthy that Edwards himself never seemed to be touched by the wild manifestations that went on in his meetings, but many of those who were closest to him were. His wife was reportedly "drunk in the Spirit" for weeks, even to the point of falling face first in her food at times.

Though Peter was certainly baptized in the Holy Spirit on the Day of Pentecost, he was apparently not touched by the manifestations that made the others appear to be drunk. When he stood up to explain the phenomena to the men of Jerusalem he said, *"These men are not drunk"* **(Acts 2:15).** Had he been personally affected he would have said "we" instead of "these men."

The spiritual seeds sown by the Cane Ridge and Red River revivals were responsible for producing the social forces that made slavery in America intolerable. In both of these movements multiplied thousands of men, women and children com-mitted their lives to the Lord. Charles Finney was just one of the mighty spiritual firebrands sparked in these revivals. The fruit of the Awakening that resulted from their ministry was great, but we, today, still have a long way to go to get as wild as the meetings from which they grew.

During the Cane Ridge and Red River revivals people coming would often be "slain in the Spirit" in their covered wagons while still miles from the camp grounds. Their horses would continue, finding their own way to the meetings, where dozens of men were assigned the task of unloading the people from the wagons and laying them in long rows until they awoke. Saplings were cut down for people to lean on while they shook so violently that the coins would fly from their pockets. Rugged pioneers would roar and bark while clinging to great trees, supposedly originating the term, "barking up a tree." Similar manifestations can be found as far back as history records renewal and revival meetings. Likewise, they all had their critics who used the same arguments against them that the present critics of this movement are using. It seems that Solomon was right—There really is nothing new under the sun.

Handling Criticism

Are these manifestations biblical? Yes. However, I do not think that the apologists for this movement will ever prove to the critics that they are. It can be a major mistake just to try to appease them. Many of the biblical prophecies that the gospel writers used to verify that Jesus was the Messiah were quite ambiguous, or obscure, and many were taken out of context. Without illumination from the Holy Spirit many of those prophecies would never be interpreted as Messianic. The opponents of the early Christians dismissed them as mis-interpretations, just as the critics of the present movement do when presented with Scriptures that verify these manifestations.

It is right to search the Scriptures for confirmation of what is happening, just as the gospel writers did, but we should do it for the sake of believers, not the for unbe-lievers. Faith is a prerequisite for receiving from God. It takes faith, not doubt, to interpret the Scriptures, or anything else, properly. There will be some "Sauls" who will be turned into "Pauls" among the opposers, but argument will never convert them. Like Saul of Tarsus they must be struck blind in the natural before they will be able to see in the Spirit.

The trap that comes when we try to satisfy the critics is that it usually takes our attention off of the Holy Spirit and where He is leading us. Soon we would be spend-ing 90% of our time trying to satisfy the 1% of the critics who would be persuaded. We must let the Lord convert the critics and keep our attention on following Him. No valid move of God is free of fault-finders, believers who really think that they are doing God a favor, just as Saul of Tarsus did before his conversion.

This is not to imply that everyone who questions a movement is sent by the enemy, or is even wrong. Many have the best of motives, but can fail to recognize what the Lord is doing for many different reasons. Even so, we must understand that the Lord does not bring correction to His church through critics, regardless of whether they call themselves watchmen, journalists, or even concerned pastors. It can be a trap to listen to anyone who does not bring correc-tion in the biblically prescribed manner, and many of those who consider them-selves the most devoted defenders of scrip-tural integrity think little of violating the

Scriptures by the way they attack others. Those who sincerely love the truth will comply with the biblical directives for bringing correction (see Matthew 18 and Galatians 6:1).

The Bereans were noble-minded because they searched the Scriptures to prove what was being taught by the apostles. They wanted to believe, not doubt. We are exhorted to, **"examine everything care-fully; hold fast to that which is *good*" (I Thessalonians 5:21),** not that which is bad. Those who examine things looking for what is wrong, wanting to doubt, will have a distorted perspective that will cause those who follow them to stumble.

The Modern Pharisees

All lovers of the Bible owe a great debt to the sect of the Pharisees. They were primarily responsible for protecting the integrity of the written Word through the centuries as it was passed down from gen-eration to generation. However, Satan is very skillful at turning our greatest strength into a weakness that he can exploit, and he did this very well with the Pharisees. He used the conservative nature that made them so protective of the Scriptures to make them into reactionaries. They began to worship the Book of the Lord more than the Lord of the Book.

When the serpent asked Eve if she could not eat from any tree in the Garden, she responded, **"from the fruit of the tree which is in the middle of the garden, God has said, 'You shall not eat from it *or touch it*, lest you die'" (Genesis 3:3).** The Lord had not said anything about "touch-ing" the fruit. Those who are overly zeal-ous for commandments are insecure and just as prone to fall as those who are overly casual about them. There is a difference between zeal that is based on love, and zealotry that is founded upon an insecure religious spirit that is seeking to gain approval through zeal. The latter is a deadly enemy of every move of God.

The religious spirit that manifested itself in the Pharisees in the Lord's day caused those who esteemed the written Word more than anyone else to persecute the One who is the personification of that Word. Those who had the greatest hope in the coming of the Messiah were those who opposed Him the most when He did not come in the form that fit into their own plans. That spirit has never left the earth, but continues to arise and oppose the Lord every time He seeks to move on the earth. To the consternation of many, this spirit usually comes in those who are zealous for the written Word, but their commitment is to the letter which kills, not the Spirit that gives life.

How should we respond to the intimidations of the modern Pharisees? Love them, pray for them, but beware of their leaven. Many of those who are delivered from this spirit, like Saul of Tarsus, can become the greatest champions of truth and the liberty of the Spirit. We should be quick to honor them for the good that they do, while boldly confronting them about their own hypocrisy.

A Movement must Keep Moving

While praying with a group of pastors in Charlotte, who were seeking the Lord about how to pastor the present movement in our city, I saw in a vision one of the leaders of the movement. He was on a horse charging forward. As he did so, a couple of bees tried to sting him. He stopped, drew his sword, and began swatting the bees with it. This was a big mistake. When he stopped he was swarmed by bees, which he would have left far behind if he had kept charging forward. The worst thing that can happen to any movement is for it to stop moving.

Another killer of movements is the pride that assumes that our movement is the greatest thing that God is doing, and that everyone who is not joining it is missing God. We have not yet discovered how to keep this mentality out of a movement, and it has probably been the main factor that has brought the end to most of the great movements in history. Pride is becoming prevalent in this movement, and to the degree that it continues to spread, it will probably dictate how long this movement lasts.

Even the biggest thing that God is doing in the earth is a small part of the whole thing that He is doing. The Scriptures attest that, **"God resists the proud, but gives grace to the humble" (James 4:6 NKJV).** It is better to have all of the demons in hell trying to stop us than to have God's opposition, and when we start to judge ourselves as superior, or others as inferior, because they are not a part of our movement, we have brought the worst form of trouble upon ourselves.

A Deadly Presumption

The ark of the covenant represented God's manifest presence to ancient Israel. When David became king it was his desire to bring the ark to Jerusalem, the seat of his government. This is the greatest wisdom that any leader can have, to provide a dwelling place for the Lord. However, David did not use wisdom in his attempt to bring in the ark with wisdom. Instead of seeking the Lord for the prescribed manner for moving the ark, he just made a new ox cart. When the cart tottered, Uzzah reached out to steady the ark. This seems like a noble thing to do, but he was struck dead for his presumption of thinking that he, in his own strength, could steady the glory of God. It is noteworthy that the ox often represents natural strength in Scripture, and Uzzah means "strength." After this incident, David regrouped and sought God to understand His prescribed manner for transporting the ark.

Our God is a holy, awesome God. He unfolds the heavens as a tent curtain. He loves us and wants to be close to us, just as He did David, *but He will be treated as holy*. When men become overly casual with His manifest presence, the results can be catastrophic. It seems that every new spiritual movement thinks that their new ox cart will be what brings in the glory of the Lord. They begin to totter, and disaster strikes.

This seems especially dangerous in this movement with all of the laughter and funny manifestations. It is easy to start thinking that He is using us because of some special gift or wisdom that we have. We should believe that if what is happening now is the prelude to a true revival, it is not coming because we are so worthy, but because we need it so badly. Revivals have historically preceded judgment. He would rather show mercy than judgment, and the only way that we will avoid judgment is to keep the revival going until the repentance and transformation that is needed to avoid judgment has been accomplished. Presumption caused the first fall from grace and most of the falls since.

We must Keep Seeking

If we measure the present movements by the standards of the great movements in history, we are swimming in very shallow waters. Even so, all of them started this way, and it is, therefore, a mistake to judge now what the ultimate impact of this movement will be. Even though there have not yet been many salvations, and no discernable social impact, in many of the great moves of God in history these have taken years to unfold. The present movements may now look like acorns compared to the great oaks of history, but every great oak started out as just such an acorn. By looking at a single seed it is not possible to know how many generations of great oak trees may ultimately come from it.

Many who miss the great moves of God do so because they get discouraged not seeing the fruit they desire mature fast enough. They fail to recognize the seeds that are to grow up into that fruit. Many of the popular teachings on the end times pressure us into expecting everything to happen very fast. I submit that God's definition of "fast" is very different from ours. He said that He was coming "quickly," and it has now been almost two thousand years. He dwells in eternity, and if we want to see from His perspective we must learn patience.

Myself and several of my prophetic friends were told back in the mid-80s that the Lord was going to pour out "the wine of His Spirit" in 1994 and 1995. I am convinced that what is now happening is what we prophesied. However, as widespread as this is becoming, it is still a very small beginning to what I was shown would ultimately unfold. What is to follow after will have much more substance and depth, but this phase is important. Let us enjoy it while we can, but be ready to move to the next phase when the time comes. ■

THE CRISIS OF HOMOSEXUALITY

BY JAMES RYLE

All Scriptures NIV unless otherwise noted.

History will have to record that the greatest tragedy of this period of social transition was not the vitriolic words and the violent actions of the bad people, but the appalling silence and indifference of the good people. Our generation will have to repent not only for the words and acts of the children of darkness, but also for the fears and apathy of the children of light.

Martin Luther King, Jr.

Introduction

It doesn't take a rocket scientist to know that something is very wrong in America—economically, politically, educationally, socially, morally and spiritually. A prophetic verse of Scripture admonishes us to **"blow the trumpet in Zion; sound the alarm on my holy hill" (Joel 2:1).** But the trumpeter must not be uncertain nor his bugle blast unclear, for **"if the trumpet does not sound a clear call, who will get ready for battle?" (I Corinthians 14:8).**

At the risk of seeming dramatic, it is with great deliberation and forethought that we must now raise the trumpet to our lips to sound the alarm on God's holy hill, against one of the desperate enemies of the truth in our time. Our prayer is that its note will pierce through the fog of confusion and cause the troops of the Lord to rally as one man—clothed in the armor of light and prepared for spiritual warfare in a day of increasing darkness.

Let me emphasize that our warfare is *spiritual*, and that the weapons of our warfare are not carnal. Our impassioned struggle is not directed against human beings, but rather against ideas, principles and entities that originate from a spiritual realm of moral darkness.

America is in the midst of a cultural revolution. We are poised on the brink of moral chaos, in danger of being pushed over the edge by the crisis of homosexuality. CRISIS is the appropriate word. It means "the point in a sickness where it is determined if the disease is in remission or terminal." What we do concerning the matter of homosexuality may determine

44 THE MORNING STAR

THE CRISIS OF HOMOSEXUALITY

whether our nation survives or dies. This is not an overstatement. One only need look through history at the fall of the Roman Empire as a case in point. The church and its leadership must come to grips with this fact: This upheaval is more than a fad—it has sufficient force and momentum to disrupt and destroy the very foundation of our society and to usher ourselves and our children into an age of godlessness and unbridled immorality.

"There is a time to be silent, and a time to speak. Now is the time to speak."

There is a time to be silent, and a time to speak. Now is the time to speak. Yet, there are some things which are difficult to talk about; more than difficult, they are indeed shameful. I frankly admit it is a delicate matter to discuss homosexuality in mixed company (for what should be obvious reasons). The Bible says, **"Have nothing to do with the fruitless deeds of darkness, but rather expose them. For it is shameful even to mention what the disobedient do in secret" (Ephesians 5:11-12).** Having the utmost regard for your moral sensitivities and tender consciences, I must proceed—for it is time to speak out on these issues and thereby expose them for what they really are.

I regard it as the sacred duty of every true pastor to care for the flock of the Lord Jesus Christ and to save His sheep from the attack of a wolf. A pastor must stand on behalf of his congregation and hold the rod of God against the tide of evil, the Word of God against the flood of lies. He must navigate his people through perilous waters with as much intelligence and as little damage as possible, bringing them to a safe haven of peace and security. This is the foremost matter on my heart as I address these issues today, avoiding indecorum as much as possible.

My immediate goal is to provide information and insight—solid answers to some very serious and complex issues. I also want to extend unquestionable compassion to anyone held in the grip of homosexual thoughts, temptations and practices. Though some remarks might seem condemnatory, due to the nature of specific issues surrounding homosexual practices, my firm intent is mercy, forgiveness and healing. May those who can be saved hear the Lord say through us: "I do not condemn you; go thy way and sin no more!" (see John 8:11).

It is very important that we also look at the bigger picture; otherwise we will become, "Crusaders of a Lesser Cause." Homosexuality is but a match ignited by the heat of a blazing forest. Sure, we can put the match out, but we had better do something about the fire in the woods! To use another metaphor, homosexuality is like a festering boil on the hide of a hideous beast. Yes, we can focus on the boil. We can treat the boil, remove the boil, medicate the boil, or cover it up with bandages—any number of possibilities are before us. But beware! Or while we are looking so intently at the boil, we just might be devoured by the beast which is alive and breathing in the earth—the beast of atheistic humanism.

Remember the Gospel

As we address these issues we must remember that our first agenda is the gospel of salvation through faith in Jesus Christ. We have been entrusted by God with the ministry of reconciliation.

Therefore, when circumstances require us to engage in the rhetorical banter of debate, we must never lose sight of the great commission given to us by the Lord Jesus to preach the Good News to everyone. Certainly we must speak the truth, but we must speak the truth in love. Paul's counsel to Timothy is well suited for us in this present cause:

> **Don't have anything to do with foolish and stupid arguments, because you know they produce quarrels.**
>
> **And the Lord's servant must not quarrel; instead, he must be kind to everyone, able to teach, not resentful.**
>
> **Those who oppose him he must gently instruct, in the hope that God will grant them repentance leading them to a knowledge of the truth,**
>
> **and that they will come to their senses and escape from the trap of the devil, who has taken them captive to do his will (II Timothy 2:23-26).**

Our ambition is to help those who are ensnared in the anguish and heartbreak caused by homosexuality to find forgiveness and freedom in Jesus Christ. But we can only do this by being honest with them about their condition and its ultimate consequences. May God grant them the wisdom to accept our helping hand as we reach out to them in love and compassion, without compromising the truth. Jesus said, **"Then you will know the truth, and the truth will set you free" (John 8:32).**

Analysis of the Facts

In the course of my research, I found numerous inaccuracies, half-truths, fallacies, and overt propaganda generated by radical elements of the homosexual community, which are presented to the general public as uncontested truth. The need to speak up became increasingly obvious with each discovery of a blatant disregard for the facts. We must speak up to separate fact from fiction.

These radical activists claim that ten percent of the population is gay, but proven research states that the figure is actually closer to one percent. They also state that all competent psychiatrists and psychologists believe homosexuality is a healthy lifestyle when, in fact, the majority in the medical community do not believe this. Gays may say that they were born homosexual, but most therapists disagree. Many also claim that they cannot change their sexual preference, but this is disproved by numerous accounts of gays who have successfully converted to heterosexuality. These and many other serious misrepresentations, which demonstrate an unmistakable, self-serving denial of truth, are rampant in the homosexual community.

Gays—An Ethnic Minority?

Perhaps the most glaring distortion of fact is the gay community's insistence that they be classified as a minority suffering from discrimination. Nothing could be further from the truth. The U.S. Supreme Court has provided definitive criteria for persons who can claim "minority" status and are, therefore, entitled to special protection and rights. Specifically, the Constitution recognizes: 1) those who as a class have suffered a history of discrimination evidenced by a lack of ability to obtain economic mean income, adequate education and cultural opportunity; 2) those who as a class exhibit obvious, immutable or distinguishing characteristics, like race, color, gender or national origin, that define them as a distinct group; and, 3) those who as a class clearly demonstrate political powerlessness.

The obvious and undeniable fact is that homosexuals do *not* meet any of these criteria. As a class they have a mean income that is 32% higher than the average American, and are more than twice as likely to have traveled outside the United States. They do not have any obvious, immutable or distinguishing characteristics. (How does one prove he is homosexual—by his skin color?) And they do not demonstrate political powerlessness, as evidenced by the homosexual protection laws that have been passed in five states and 90 countries—some of which actually restrict the religious freedom and free speech rights of other citizens.

Homosexuals may say and do whatsoever they please against others—all in the name of freedom of speech—with no repercussions! Yet, those who would speak out are held hostage to silence by threats of boycott, vandalism, verbal abuse and harassment. (It is disgraceful to watch politicians cower and cater to homosexuals out of fear of having them as political enemies!) Let's not insult those with legitimate claims of discrimination by including homosexuals in the same category. As one black pastor stated, "The bus that went to Selma was never meant to go to Sodom!"

A Clever Twisting of Language

Besides distorting facts, there is also deceptive twisting of language that diverts the focus from the real and serious issues regarding homosexuality, and engages the public in debate over abstract social questions and idealogies. For example, porno-graphic images are now called "art" and subsidized by government grants. Indecent exposure in public is now called "freedom of speech" and is protected by the Bill of Rights. The term "homophobia" is employed to suggest that normal, healthy people are somehow afflicted by a pathological condition when they express revulsion for the so-called "gay" lifestyle. And the term "gay" itself, once upon a time a simple adjective evocative of innocence and joy, is now a term denoting a chosen lifestyle of deviant sensuality. Anyone who seeks to know the truth about homosexuality will discover there is in fact nothing "gay" about it at all!

Moreover, the shameful and shocking sexual practices of homosexuals are deliberately down-played to keep public sentiment from turning against them in honest revulsion. Some homosexuals would actually have us believe that their relationships with one another have nothing to do with sex at all! In an attempt to shift our focus away from the "sex issue," homosexuals have cleverly taken "discrimination" as their theme, knowing all too well that the sympathies of the American mainstream have generally favored the oppressed. Any expression of disapproval toward homosexuality is interpreted as discrimination. This is yet another example of the distortion of fact. When anyone attempts to confront or correct homosexual thought or practice, the airwaves are filled with cries of "censorship and totalitarian repression." Inflammatory charges to be sure; yet it is homosexual themselves who are the most implacable censors of all. No one dares to disagree with them under the threat of harassment, assault and lawsuit. How preposterous it is that we risk being labeled self-righteous bigots simply for saying these things!

Colorado is now called the "Hate State" because of the controversy over Amendment 2. This is not a discrimination issue. According to the State Attorney General, Gale Norton, in a report filed by law: "The amendment has only the intent and effect of establishing a statewide policy of governmental neutrality with respect to sexual orientation . . . it does not deprive homosexuals or bisexuals of the protection provided for all citizens. It simply provides that homosexuals or bi-sexual orientation should not be granted *special* protection."

Despite this fact, the homosexual movement and the liberal media seek to confuse the issue by insisting their civil rights are being threatened. Homosexuals prove yet again that the Scripture's indictment of them is accurate: they **"suppress the truth in unrighteousness" (Romans 1:18).** Indeed, their only claim to legitimacy is found by making everything else look illegitimate!

What about AIDS?

Even more alarming is the coverup surrounding the deadly and ever-increasing AIDS epidemic. Homosexuals try to portray AIDS as a civil rights issue when, in truth, the disease is a public health issue. We are being misled by those who promote civil rights rhetoric and misplaced tolerance as the politically correct response both to the HIV/AIDS threat, and to those who are most responsible for it—homosexuals. Prudent concern for public health and common-sense moral prohibitions are the correct stance in the face of this growing plague that now threatens innocent bystanders.

The *New England Journal of Medicine*, the *Journal of the American Medical Association*, and other prestigious periodicals give ample evidence that standard gay activities are not merely unsanitary and offensive deviations of behavior, but such practices are also horrendous assaults on the physical health of individuals who engage in them. Homosexual activities cause massive immunological disruptions in the blood, as well as serious trauma to the body. AIDS itself was initially called GRID—Gay Related Immune Deficiency. Current figures indicate that 70% of the nation's AIDS cases involve male homosexuals or bisexuals.

Tragically, the careless behavior of these individuals has made the disease a monstrous public health menace for all! It threatens not only our physical well-being, but also our financial security as well. Because of the AIDS epidemic, you and I now subsidize homosexual irresponsibility with higher insurance rates across the board. Yet, homosexuals want to silence our right to hold them accountable for the consequences of their immorality—even when those consequences seriously affect us.

Why be so outspoken on these things? There is a time to be silent, and a time to speak. Now is the time to speak. Nevertheless, there are inherent risks in speaking out on such a volatile issue. The blatant disdain for truth exhibited by angry homosexuals stirs even the most compassionate among us with a sense of urgency in our defense of righteousness, truth, and healthy living. Our zeal is viewed by the homosexual community as homophobic hostility, hatred and bigotry. It is in fact none of these, but it serves their purpose for them to say that we are "gaybashing," because it inflames public sentiment and diverts attention away from the truth.

A physician would be guilty of malpractice if he didn't warn someone with a serious condition simply because he did not want to hurt his feelings. The most loving act one can do is to point out when a harmful abnormality exists, and offer help. This needs to be done with homosexuality, but not in a spirit of condemnation. The most serious mistake that we as individuals could make right now is to cater to the homosexual agenda and leave them to believe that they are all right—that their lifestyle is recognized and accepted as a normal and healthy alternative to heterosexuality. Such a stand would not only condemn homosexuals to a horrible death but would, in fact, endanger the very future of this nation! We must tell them an abnormality exists and help them with everything we have to find healing and forgiveness through Jesus Christ!

The Biblical Perspective

Ecclesiastes 7:29 states: **"This only have I found: God made mankind upright, but men have gone in search of many schemes [have sought out many inventions]" (KJV).** The Hebrew word used for "upright" (*yaw-shar'*) means "straight, righteous, pleasant, or prosperous." The word used for "schemes" or "inventions" (*khaw-shab'*) means "to weave or to fabricate; to plot, contrive, imagine or devise in a malicious sense." The world is filled with the malicious inventions of fallen man. Homosexuality is one such "invention," and that is what I seek to demonstrate. Solomon gave us a glimpse of how it started: **"God made mankind upright."** The apostle Paul, in II Timothy 3:1-17, gave us a prophetic forecast of how it will all end. Paul's exhortation gives us three basic thoughts, the first of which is *the dreadful revelation of how far man has fallen*:

> **But mark this: There will be terrible times in the last days.**
>
> **People will be lovers of themselves, lovers of money, boastful, proud, abusive, disobedient to their parents, ungrateful, unholy,**
>
> **without love, unforgiving, slanderous, without self-control, brutal, not lovers of the good,**
>
> **treacherous, rash, conceited, lovers of pleasure rather than lovers of God—**
>
> **having a form of godliness but denying its power. Have nothing to do with them . . .**
>
> **so also these men oppose the truth—men of depraved minds, who, as far as the faith is concerned, are rejected.**
>
> **But they will not get very far because, as in the case of those men, their folly will be clear to everyone.**

Paul's second theme is *the certainty of persecution against those who are godly*:

> **You, however, know all about my teaching, my way of life, my purpose, faith, patience, love, endurance,**
>
> **persecutions, sufferings—what kinds of things happened to me in Antioch, Iconium and Lystra, the persecutions I endured. Yet the Lord rescued me from all of them.**
>
> **In fact, everyone who wants to live a godly life in Christ Jesus will be persecuted,**
>
> **while evil men and impostors will go from bad to worse, deceiving and being deceived.**

Paul's third main point is *a call for faithfulness*:

But as for you, continue in what you have learned and have become convinced of, because you know those from whom you learned it,

and how from infancy you have known the holy Scriptures, which are able to make you wise for salvation through faith in Christ Jesus.

All Scripture is God-breathed and is useful for teaching, rebuking, correcting and training in righteousness,

so that the man of God may be thoroughly equipped for every good work.

The rejection of God and truth brings dire consequences, as we read in Romans 1:18-32:

The wrath of God is being revealed from heaven against all the godlessness and wickedness of men who suppress the truth by their wickedness,

since what may be known about God is plain to them, because God has made it plain to them.

For since the creation of the world God's invisible qualities—his eternal power and divine nature—have been clearly seen, being understood from what has been made, so that men are without excuse.

For although they knew God, they neither glorified him as God nor gave thanks to him, but their thinking became futile and their foolish hearts were darkened.

Although they claimed to be wise, they became fools

and exchanged the glory of the immortal God for images made to look like mortal man and birds and animals and reptiles.

It is important to note that God's wrath is not against those who do not *know* the truth, but against those who *suppress* it. We can see in this text the five steps that lead to God's wrath: 1) rejecting God, 2) suppressing truth, 3) embracing wickedness, 4) practicing evil and 5) worshiping idols. It is also interesting to note from the following text that the wrath of God *abandons man to himself.*

Therefore God gave them over in the sinful desires of their hearts to sexual impurity for the degrading of their bodies with one another.

They exchanged the truth of God for a lie, and worshiped and served created things rather than the Creator—who is forever praised. Amen.

Because of this, God gave them over to shameful lusts. Even their women exchanged natural relations for unnatural ones.

In the same way the men also abandoned natural relations with women and were inflamed with lust for one another. Men committed indecent acts with other men, and received in themselves the due penalty for their perversion.

The great tragedy today is that most people in the general population do not really understand what the homosexual lifestyle really involves. The present liberal media will not tell us. Children in schools are being indoctrinated in sex education classes with the idea that homosexuality is simply an alternative lifestyle. Homosexuals are brought into classes to show that they are mostly successful businessmen, lawyers and doctors, which many are; but the purpose is to show themselves as victims of homophobia. Most

Americans would be highly offended if they really understood what was going on, what their children are being taught, or, more accurately, what they're NOT being taught about homosexuality.

The Due Penalties

Paul elaborated on just what the due penalties are for those who are "given over" in verses 28-32:

> **Furthermore, since they did not think it worthwhile to retain the knowledge of God, he gave them over to a depraved mind, to do what ought not to be done.**
>
> **They have become filled with every kind of wickedness, evil, greed and depravity. They are full of envy, murder, strife, deceit and malice. They are gossips,**
>
> **slanderers, God-haters, insolent, arrogant and boastful; they invent ways of doing evil; they disobey their parents;**
>
> **they are senseless, faithless, heartless, ruthless.**
>
> **Although they know God's righteous decree that those who do such things deserve death, they not only continue to do these very things but also approve of those who practice them.**

These penalties can be listed as: 1) depraved in their minds, 2) filled with every kind of wickedness, 3) deceitful in their behavior, 4) disobedient to authority and 5) defiant against God. Just what is happening to our modern society? All of these are not only present, they are increasing at a frightening rate.

Conclusions

There is an abnormality. The vast majority of people know that homosexuality is wrong. Our compassion for those ensnared by the deception of their condition compels us to respond by speaking the truth to all who will hear. We cannot let their passionate (though highly illogical) arguments sway us from the obvious fact that homosexuality is *wrong*.

It is time to speak and draw the line. Neutrality on this subject is impossible. Left unattended it will destroy society by redefining moral, family and civil law. We must confront the issues with truth and sanity. John Wesley said, "Making an open stand against all the ungodliness and unrighteousness which overspread our land as a flood, is one of the noblest ways of confessing Christ in the face of His enemies." My father had a saying, "Silence isn't always golden; sometimes its just plain yellow." These words of an old hymn have long been a favorite of mine in calling for courageous faith and action in a day of increasing darkness:

> *Once to every man and nation,*
> *comes the moment to decide*
> *In the strife of truth with falsehood,*
> *for the good or evil side.*
> *Some great cause, some great decision,*
> *offering each the bloom or blight.*
> *And that choice goes by forever*
> *between that darkness and the light.*
> *Then it is the brave man chooses,*
> *while the coward stands aside*
> *Until the multitude makes virtue*
> *of a faith they had denied.*
> *—James Russel Lowell, 1819-1891*

We must draw the line and take a decisive stand against the immoral and destructive power of homosexual lust; not just for ourselves, but especially for our children. If we do not draw the line here, then exactly where will we draw it? At what point will we stand and say, "That is enough!" Uncensored pornography? Child-molestation? Public nudity? Unchallenged sex acts in the park? Rape? Sadomasochism? Murder? Be well advised that the homosexual agenda, left to run its course, will open the door for every one of these. Already in countries like Sweden and New Zealand, adult consent laws have been successfully overturned, making sex with children legal, providing that the child first consents! Such is what happens when just men do nothing.

If we yield under the pressure of "political correctness" and public opinion on this matter of homosexuality and by our silence concede, then what will we say to the next "issue" that comes along? And there are many such "issues" waiting in the wings. If the foolish argument being used by homosexuals can win the day for them, then there is no logical reason to assume that these other newly-labeled "ethnic groups" will not use the same line of argument for their own "preferences." So, if we do not take a stand here, then where will we stand? If we do not speak up now, then when will we speak?

We must Bring Healing

We must bring the healing of Christ to those men and women who are ensnared in the horrors of homosexuality. But we can only bring true healing by being truthful with our assessment of the condition. The Good News is that forgiveness and healing are sufficient and available through Jesus Christ.

Healing for the Homosexual

Do you not know that the wicked will not inherit the kingdom of God? Do not be deceived: Neither the sexually immoral nor idolaters nor adulterers nor male prostitutes nor homosexual offenders

nor thieves nor the greedy nor drunkards nor slanderers nor swindlers will inherit the kingdom of God.

And that is what some of you were. But you were washed, you were sanctified, you were justified in the name of the Lord Jesus Christ and by the Spirit of our God (I Corinthians 6:9-11).

This passage of Scripture lists a host of immoralities, including homosexuality, and shows the inevitable and eternal consequences of continuing in these practices. While the Bible tells it like it is, it certainly does not speak in what has become characteristically regarded as self-righteous puritanism. It is neither condescending nor condemnatory. Rather, it offers great hope to anyone who wants recovery and lasting freedom from the grip of sin:

That is what some of you were. But you were washed, you were sanctified, you were justified in the name of the Lord Jesus Christ and by the Spirit of our God.

This is what we hope to accomplish, specifically as it pertains to homosexuals.

Yet, while we are being specific, we are not being exclusive. For *all* have sinned and fall short of the glory of God. It is very doubtful that there is anyone who has never had a lustful thought that deviated from God's perfect ideal of sexuality. We are all human beings made in the likeness and image of God, yet fallen, with all the glory and tragedy which that paradox implies, including sexual potential and sexual problems. In light of this, John Stott's words ring true with compassion and wisdom: "However strongly we may disapprove of homosexual practices, we have no liberty to dehumanize those who engage in them."

The Moral Conflict

No aspect of the contemporary sexual revolution has been more talked about and caused more anguish than the issue of homosexuality. The constant and biased attention given to the subject unquestionably contributes to the impression that homosexuality is omnipresent when in fact it is merely concentrated in certain places with high visibility, giving the illusion of prevalence. The truth is that the problem is not as widespread, nor as generally accepted, as we are being led to believe.

Still, it is a very serious problem. We have been bombarded by the vocal and vindictive pro-homosexual movement with its cries for total tolerance and acceptance, and its senseless threats of boycott against any display of disagreement. They feel strongly that they are the last oppressed minority in America. But that is a lie, just as homosexuality itself is a lie. But once the lie is believed, acting out the corresponding behavior is somewhat understandable, though not acceptable. And thus we have one side of the conflict.

The other side of the conflict calls for the total rejection of the homosexual problem and expresses an unwillingness to face it in any plausible way. Some religious conservatives denounce not only homosexuality, but also condemn homosexuals themselves with a passionate hatred. Such a posture forecloses any hope of escape for those ensnared in homosexuality, and virtually nullifies the gospel's intent of being "good news." Others, less given to religious passions, show their prejudice through apathy, allowing homosexuality to run its course and in the end destroy itself. The great majority of us are caught in the crossfire of these two equally unacceptable extremes.

The Real Issues

The most important issues involved in homosexuality must be dealt with. These are the issues of its cause and origin, and the question of possible change in both homosexual orientation and behavior. The possibility of change is of great interest because of the obvious failure of the homosexual lifestyle to provide a truly gay and happy experience. On the contrary, the homosexual way of living, even quite independent from the glaring medical consequence, has been extremely damaging for those who have sought fulfillment in its hollow promises. Homosexuality offers nothing but a horrifying desperation. Despite the glamorized images portrayed by the irresponsible liberal media, the lifestyle of homosexuals is not as "gay" as it is made out to be.

Homosexuality is represented in the media in a slanted, rose-colored-glass way. That may be understandable as propaganda, but if one hears the life stories of practicing homosexuals over the course of many years, it becomes clear that happiness is not found in that way of life. Restlessness in their contacts, loneliness, jealousy, neurotic depressions, venereal amid other physical diseases, suicides: that is the other side of the coin *not* being shown by the media. Indeed the media will not show the whole picture. There is a great amount of vital and available information all but barred from publicity due to the prejudice of pro-homosexual liberals who censure unwelcome views.

Former Homosexuals Speak Out

One man admits, "In spite of the outward appearance, homosexuality always ends in despair." Another says, "It's a rough world, and I wouldn't wish it on my worse enemy. Over the years I've lived with a succession of roommates, some of whom I professed to love. They swore that they loved me. But homosexual ties begin and end with sex. There is so little else to go on. After that first passionate fling, sex becomes less and less frequent. The partners become nervous. They want new thrills, new experiences. They begin to cheat on each other—secretly at first, then more obviously. There are jealous rages and fights. Eventually you split up and begin hustling around for a new lover." Summarizing it in yet another way, journalist Doris Hanson stated, "The homosexual lifestyle consists of a world where emotions are built on lies. To achieve momentary gratification from sex, homosexuals say 'I love you' as often as they say 'good morning.' Once the experience is over they are only too ready to say 'goodbye.' And the chase begins again."

Explaining what "homosexual love" really is, understandably, often meets with indignant resistance. "Why am I not allowed to become happy the way I am?" is the predictable dramatic cry. The question, however, is not whether or not it is allowed, but whether or not it is viable. The undeniable fact is that a large number of homosexuals are very unhappy with their lives. When they learn that they are homosexual, almost *all* homosexuals are appalled and depressed by this knowledge.

The homosexual lifestyle breeds enormous guilt over sexual promiscuity, over constant lies about permanent loving relationships that are actually broken within weeks, sometimes within days, even hours (after the encounter). This guilt, along with dashed hopes of being heterosexual, weighs heavily upon homosexuals—ultimately giving place to a depressing fatalism: "I am just this way, and nothing can be done about it!" This self-pity invariably engenders feelings of protest, whether in the form of anger, hostility, rebelliousness, or bitterness—because the individual feels unjustly treated through the failure of others to understand and accept them as they are.

Now some may ask, "Isn't that the effect of social discrimination?" The plain and truthful answer is "no." It is true that the homosexually-oriented are not really considered normal by others, but the main cause of their feeling tragically different and rejected lies deep within themselves. These people retain this feeling even when they live in an accepting environment. This is why, ultimately, no amount of acceptance or affirmation will ever satisfy their hunger for approval—the problem is on the *inside* of them, and can only be healed by an inside job! And that is what Jesus Christ offers to all who have sinned!

"All have sinned and fall short of the glory of God" (Romans 3:23). Let's go easy on dishing out condemnation, for we just might have to eat the meal ourselves. Yes, homosexuality is a sin, for it "misses the mark" of the glory for which God created man. But, then, so does alcoholism, compulsive gambling, drug abuse, lying and cheating, pride and self-righteousness, and a host of assorted "phobias" and other untold sexual disorders such as chronic masturbation, pornographic addiction, adultery, fornication. Perhaps the glaring silence of the moral majority is a self-indictment. After all, how can we confront one sin while we are so deeply engaged in practicing the others? Then is silence the answer? No! We cannot shrug our shoulders and accept homosexuality as just another thing. Silence at this time would be the most sinister form of discrimination possible. For it would effectively consign homosexuals to the desperation of that lifestyle and deliver them ultimately to an untimely and horrible death. The proverb says, **"Discipline your son, for in that there is hope; do not be a willing party to his death [by standing by and doing nothing]" (Proverbs 19:18).** Compassion joins forces with conviction and compels us to speak to the crisis of homosexuality. As for our own guilt in the matter of other sins, the recourse is clear. Let us all turn to Christ, forsake sinful behavior and love one another as God intended!

Forgiveness and healing for homosexuality, as with any sin, are only possible when we admit that it is sin. Homosexuality is not what God intends, nor is it what man was created for. It is wrong—morally, physically, emotionally and socially. It is far short of the glory of God and well beneath the dignity of man. But, with repentance, a glorious and profound change is possible!

This is not to imply that change is instantaneous, nor that those who embrace Christ do not struggle with the recurrence of temptation and possible relapse into old habits. More often than not the change

occurs deep within the individual in an instant, but requires a lifetime of responsible choices, now made because of the individual's freedom from sin's power through the indwelling power of the Holy Spirit. Christ gives each of us the threefold grace of faith, hope and love. *Faith* to accept and maintain His standards, *Hope* to look beyond the present suffering to future glory, and *Love* to care for and support one another. These are God's guarantees for our victory.

But why does the particular sin of homosexuality sit upon certain individuals? Why single them out? What is the access point that opens them to something anyone would dread? What are the causes of homosexual orientation? Some are as follows: 1) The breakdown of healthy families, 2) rejection, isolation and loneliness, 3) absence of nurturing and 4) the addictive power of lust.

What about the claim: "I didn't choose to be a homosexual!"? Though this may meet with some controversy, it is true that the majority of homosexuals are in fact not responsible for their condition. Yet, while they are not responsible for their condition, they *are* responsible for their conduct! Indeed, all of us are. What Jesus Christ offers to homosexuals is both rational and realistic. You can be changed! You do not have to live in the belief that there is nothing you can do about your condition! Jesus offers the only solution, and He gives it without rebuke or condemnation.

When the woman was caught in sexual sin, the Lord asked, **"Where are those thine accusers?"** Then He said, **"Neither do I condemn thee: go, and sin no more" (John 8:10-11 KJV).** This story is one of the greatest examples of the magnificence and mercy of Jesus Christ toward one who is sexually broken. There is no condemnation for those who are in Christ (see Romans 8:1).

This brings us to the possibility and promise of *change!* I Corinthians 6:11 reads,

And such were some of you; but you were washed, but you were sanctified, but you were justified in the name of the Lord Jesus Christ, and in the Spirit of our God (NAS).

Being washed is to have our sins fully remitted. Being sanctified is to be made holy. Being justified is to be rendered innocent. These words hold great promise for *all* who suffer under the bitter anguish of homosexuality. The power of homosexuality can be broken, and the effects removed from one's thoughts and behavior. But, *how* is this possible? In the name of the Lord Jesus Christ, and by the power of the Holy Spirit.

II Corinthians 5:17 says that, *"if anyone is in Christ, he is a new creation;* **the old has gone, the new has come!"** Being born again makes it possible for us to start all over—no matter who we were or what we've done.

Paul's testimony came from personally being changed by the power of the gospel. In I Timothy 1:15-16 he said,

Here is a trustworthy saying that deserves full acceptance: Christ Jesus came into the world to save sinners—of whom I am the worst.

But for that very reason I was shown mercy so that in me, the worst of sinners, Christ Jesus might display his unlimited patience as an example for those who would believe on him and receive eternal life.

In Philippians 3:13-14 he further stated,

Brothers, I do not consider myself yet to have taken hold of it. But one thing I do: Forgetting what is behind and straining toward what is ahead,

I press on toward the goal to win the prize for which God has called me heavenward in Christ Jesus.

Later he continued, **"I can do everything through** *him who gives* **me strength" (Philippians 4:13).**

The Healing Role of Community

The first thing that God said was not good was for man to be alone (see Genesis 2:18). God created us to live with one another. Independence and isolation separate us from God's purpose and open us to the counterfeits and substitutes provided by Satan. When we come to Jesus, He brings us out of the death caused by sin and places us back into a healing community. This truth was illustrated dramatically when Jesus raised Lazarus from the dead. He called Lazarus to come out, then He commanded that he be released from his grave clothes. He is doing the same for homosexuals today: calling them to come out of the grave and be released that they might walk in resurrection life.

For the Love of a Father

Consider this conclusion of a psychiatrist: "After having a great many contacts with homosexually afflicted men in the course of my professional life I have observed that in not one single case has there been a normal, loving father/son relationship!" This is the great tragedy of homosexuality. The following is a poem I

FOR THE LOVE OF A FATHER by James Ryle

There was a boy who never knew the love a father gives,
Raised by his mom in anger for the man who left his kids.
The moment came in growing up when gates were opened wide,
And the boy, whose heart was wounded, walked into the other side.
His appetite for nurture to be given by a man
Had been left an empty vacuum as he roamed about the land.
He tried to stroke himself in closets, hidden from the light,
But it never satisfied him so he wandered into night.
Looking for the man who would make him feel complete,
He gave himself to do such things that some would never speak.
It always started out with hope that love would finally heal,
But each encounter broke him more and left him feeling ill.

Dying for affection which he wrongly sought in man
He turned for help to others thinking they would understand.
Instead they told him Sodom burned for such things he had done
"How could you hurt your family so? You're such a sorry son!"
Angered by the social pride that turns from darker things,
The lad now swore to desecrate the palaces of kings.
He bound himself in common cause with others such as he
Who had suffered long the anguish of their public mockery.

Parades were formed and marches made to show their new defiance.
Hand in hand, in open view, they stood a bold alliance.
Supposing this would win the day and give them what they needed,
They entered into loud debate and publicly they pleaded.
"Equal rights! We are deprived! Treat us true and fair!
Your moral rules are meaningless, for them we do not care!"
The rhetoric, inflamed by fear, polarized their cause;
Civil strife erupted through the breaking of God's Laws.
What they had hoped would give them peace instead provoked a war,
And a nation, known for tolerance, these things do now abhor.
And the boy who never knew the love and kindness of a father
Died a victim of disease; alone, with no one who would bother.

The answer to this problem lies within the heart of those
Who are filled with Christ's compassion for the travelers on the road.
We can heal their broken bodies and restore their fallen hearts
If we'll only stop from judging them for how they fell apart.

The little boy who never knew, and yet became a man,
Can feel the love of Christ in you if you will touch his hand.
Help him to recover from the darkness of his fall,
For the love of God gives freedom unto any who will call.

To the homosexual Jesus promised:

Come to me, all you who are weary and burdened, and I will give you rest.

Take my yoke upon you and learn from me, for I am gentle and humble in heart, and you will find rest for your souls.

For my yoke *is easy* and my burden is light (Matthew 11:28-30).

Jesus is the Wonderful Counselor who understands your deepest and darkest sin. Jesus is the Mighty God who destroys the power of your dreadful enemy. Jesus is the Everlasting Father who holds you in His eternal arms of unfailing love. Jesus is the Prince of Peace who fulfills your life with lasting relationships.

Summary

I have dealt in a very direct way with the crisis of homosexuality and how to provide healing for homosexuals. I was obligated to say certain things which needed to be said, but which are also somewhat controversial. Some comments might seem condemnatory. That is, however, not my intent. I have simply spoken the truth in love in hope that the truth can be known, love can be experienced, and healing and freedom can be the results. In light of the potential consequence of such candid preaching, I would like to refer to a verse which I find particularly relevant: **"I am a man of peace; but when I speak, they are for war" (Psalm 120:7).**

Jesus said, **"Blessed are the peacemakers, for they will be called sons of God" (Matthew 5:9).** I am a peacemaker, as any Christian is. As a peacemaker, I long to see reconciliation in all broken relationships. Not only the relationships broken from man to God, but also the relationships broken horizontally, man to man. The gospel is the power of God unto salvation for anyone who believes—whether Jew or Gentile, male or female, Greek or barbarian, bond or free. As a peacemaker, I seriously try to be **"all things to all men so that by all possible means I might save some" (I Corinthians 9:22).** I am for healing, yet there are some who are for war. The reasons are obvious: Some topics are so inherently controversial as to make peace a virtual impossibility.

Homosexuality is one such topic. Our Christian view on this matter—the perspective given in Holy Scripture which reflects the opinion of Almighty God—is diametrically opposed to the contemporary world view fostered and fashioned by atheistic humanism. Everything we say is directly against what is currently advanced as the politically correct agenda. They would have us agree or say nothing at all. We can do neither. We cannot be silent because of the consequences of that silence. We cannot agree, because what is being proposed is wrong. It is not just simply an aberrant form of life. It is— when you know the truth—an abomination. Therefore, we must speak about it. We must speak about it with love, but we must speak about it truthfully. That is the only hope for finding any positive solution to the crisis.

However, even as we speak for peace our words are used as an occasion for strife and aggression. In fact, it seems inevitable that we will endure opposition. Jesus Himself experienced it: **"Consider him that endured such contradiction of sinners against himself, lest ye be wearied and faint in your minds" (Hebrews 12:3).** The Greek word for "contradiction" literally means "anti-logic." Jesus endured illogical assumptions that were so outrageous, no one in their right mind could honestly hold these positions. When someone is challenged by truth they do not want to accept, their only option is to combat it with nonsense. If nonsense is spoken with enough passion, enough power, enough presence and bearing, it can be touted as a plausible reality. But, in fact, it is (and always will be) *non*-sense. When we step back and take an objective, common sense approach to the tenets of the homosexual agenda, we can only conclude that it is nonsense. We cannot leave those who are caught up in it to believe that it is true. Therefore we must speak the truth.

Why Peace Instead of War

The Bible says,

Therefore, since we have been justified through faith, we have peace with God through our Lord Jesus Christ,

through whom we have gained access by faith into this grace in which we now stand. And we rejoice in the hope of the glory of God (Romans 5:1-2).

Because we have had peace given to us, we are peacemakers—so that all men and women everywhere, in every nation, might know the peace that passes understanding; might taste and see that the Lord is good and might have the war that rages in their souls ended by the peace of the Lord's kingdom. Yet, when we speak there are some who will take our words and turn them into an occasion for strife and battle.

We must remember that we wrestle not against flesh and blood, but against principalities, powers, rulers of darkness, and spiritual wickedness in high places (see Ephesians 6:12 KJV). The weapons of our warfare are not carnal, but mighty through God to the pulling down of strongholds (see II Corinthians 10:4 KJV). As it relates to those humans who are afflicted, oppressed and victimized by Satan's agenda, we have the most awesome weapon known in the history of humanity. It is love. It is the mercy of God that has provided us with so great a salvation and brought us peace with God and with one another. Our position is one of redemption, reclamation and forgiveness, because of the mercy of the Lord. As Christians we profoundly believe that the power of the grace of God is greater than any yoke of bondage that the enemy can place on a person.

Mercy is an activity in which God engages Himself for the purpose of forgiving, restoring, changing and blessing those to whom He is committed. Mercy is not only the withholding of deserved punishment; it is also the abundant bestowal of undeserved blessings. There are two great facts that we must never forget about God's mercy: All men are in desperate need of it, and the Lord has enough for all men. ■

This is a condensed version of a series taught by James Ryle. The complete series is available on tape, with an accompanying study guide that covers this subject in much greater detail. For more information call 1-800-453-5158 or write: A Time to Speak, 7845 Lookout Road, Longmont, CO 80503. James Ryle is the senior pastor of the Boulder, Colorado Vineyard Church. James is well-known for his prophetic accuracy and insight into the ways of the Spirit. A popular conference speaker, James may be contacted at the Boulder Vineyard at the above address.

THE HORDES OF HELL ARE MARCHING

PART I

by

RICK JOYNER

PROPHECY

On February the 16th, 1995 I was given a dream in which I saw a great army from hell that had been released against the church. Two days later I was given a vision in which I saw this diabolical horde again, but in much greater detail. This is an abbreviated version of the first part of that vision. The second part will appear in the next edition of the Journal.

There are some aspects of this vision that were honestly repulsive, but I have tried to share it just the way I saw it. The works of darkness are repulsive in the most profound sense of that word, and we must recognize them as such.

In the first part of this vision I saw the degree to which this evil has its grip on believers, how many Christians are being used by the enemy, and what it will take to set them free. In the second part of the vision I saw a unified, glorious church rise up as a great army in the most pivotal battle of all time between light and darkness. This battle is already beginning to rage. Dreams and visions are usually metaphorical, and this one definitely is. Even so, what it represents is real, and is happening now. It was for this reason I decided to share it in this abbreviated form, even though it may at times seem incomplete. If you hear the Lord's voice through this vision, do not harden your heart. Put on the whole armor of God, and prepare for the battle.

The Evil Army

I saw a demonic army so large that it stretched as far as I could see. It was separated into divisions, with each carrying a different banner. The foremost and most powerful divisions were Pride, Self-righteousness, Respectability, Selfish Ambition, and Unrighteous Judgment, but the largest of all was Jealousy. The leader of this vast army was the Accuser of the Brethren himself. I knew that there were many more evil divisions beyond my scope of vision, but these were the vanguard of this terrible horde from hell that was now being released against the church.

The weapons carried by this horde had names on them: the swords were named Intimidation; the spears were named Treachery; and their arrows were named Accusations, Gossip, Slander and Faultfinding. Scouts and smaller companies of demons with such names as Rejection, Bitterness, Impatience, Unforgiveness and Lust were sent in advance of this army to prepare for the main attack. I knew in my heart that the church had never faced anything like this before.

The main assignment of this army was to cause division. It was sent to attack every level of relationship— churches with each other, congregations with their pastors, husbands and wives, children and parents, and even children with each other. The scouts were sent to locate the openings in churches, families or individuals that rejection, bitterness, lust, etc., could exploit and make a larger breech for the divisions that were coming.

> *"The most shocking part of this vision was that this horde was not riding on horses, but on Christians!"*

The most shocking part of this vision was that this horde was not riding on horses, but on Christians! Most of them were well-dressed, respectable, and had the appearance of being refined and educated. These were Christians who had opened themselves to the powers of darkness to such a degree that the enemy could use them and they would think they were being used by God. The Accuser knows that a house divided cannot stand, and this army represented his ultimate attempt to bring such complete division to the church that she would completely fall from grace.

The Prisoners

Trailing behind these first divisions were a vast multitude of other Christians who were prisoners of this army. They were all wounded, and were guarded by little demons of Fear. There seemed to be more prisoners than there were demons in the army. Surprisingly, these prisoners still had their swords and shields, but they did not use them. It was shocking to see that so many could be kept captive by so few of these little demons of Fear. These could have easily been destroyed or driven off if the prisoners had just used their weapons.

Above the prisoners the sky was black with vultures named Depression. These would land on the shoulders of a prisoner and vomit on him. The vomit was Condemnation. When the vomit hit a prisoner he would stand up and march a little straighter for a while, and then slump over, even weaker than before. Again, I wondered why the prisoners did not simply kill these vultures with their swords, which they could have easily done.

Occasionally a weak prisoner would stumble and fall. As soon as he or she hit the ground, the other prisoners would begin stabbing them with their swords, scorning them as they did so. They would then call for the vultures to begin devouring the fallen one even before they were dead.

As I watched, I realized that these prisoners thought that the vomit of Condemnation was truth from God. Then I understood that these prisoners actually thought they were marching in the army of God! This is why they did not kill the little demons of fear, or the vultures—they thought these were messengers from God! The darkness from the cloud of vultures made it so hard for these prisoners to see that they naively accepted everything that happened to them as being from the Lord.

The only food provided for these prisoners was the vomit from the vultures. Those who refused to eat it simply weakened until they fell. Those who did eat it were strengthened, but with the strength of the evil one. They would then begin to vomit on the others. When one began to do this a demon that was waiting for a ride would be given this one and he or she would be promoted to the front divisions.

Even worse than the vomit from the vultures was a repulsive slime that these demons were urinating and defecating upon the Christians they rode. This slime was the pride, selfish ambition, etc., that was the nature of the division they were a part of. However, this slime made the Christians feel so much better than the condemnation that they easily believed that the demons were messengers of God, and they actually thought this slime was the anointing of the Holy Spirit.

"They actually thought this slime was the anointing of the Holy Spirit."

Then the voice of the Lord came to me saying, *"This is the beginning of the enemy's last day army. This is Satan's ultimate deception, and his ultimate power of destruction is released when he uses Christians to attack other Christians. Throughout the ages he has used this army, but never has he been able to capture so many to be used for his evil purposes. Do not fear. I have an army too. You must now stand and fight, because there is no longer any place to hide from this war. You must fight for My kingdom, for truth, and for those who have been deceived."*

I had been so repulsed and outraged by the evil army that I had wanted to die rather than live in such a world. However, this word from the Lord was so encouraging that I immediately began yelling to the Christian prisoners that they were deceived, thinking that they would listen to me. When I did this, it seemed that the whole army turned to look at me, but I kept yelling. I thought that the Christians were going to wake up and realize what was happening to them, but instead many of them started reaching for their arrows to shoot at me. The others just hesitated as if they did not know what to make of me. I knew then that I had done this prematurely, and that it had been a very foolish mistake.

The Battle Begins

Then I turned and saw the army of the Lord standing behind me. There were thousands of soldiers, but we were still greatly outnumbered. Only a small number were fully dressed in their armor so that most were only partially protected. A large number were already wounded. Most of those who had all of their armor still had very small shields which I knew would not protect them from the onslaught that was coming. The majority of these soldiers were women and children.

Behind this army there was a trailing mob similar to the prisoners who followed the evil army, but very different in nature. These seemed to be very happy people, and were playing games, singing songs, feasting and roaming about from one little camp to the next. It reminded me of the atmosphere at Woodstock. I tried to raise my voice above the clamor to warn them that it was not the time for this, that the battle was about to begin, but only a few could even hear my voice. Those who did gave me the "peace sign" and said they did not believe in war, and that the Lord would not let anything bad happen to them. I tried to explain that the Lord had given us armor for a reason, but they just retorted that they had come to a place of peace and joy where nothing would happen to them. I began praying earnestly for the Lord to increase the faith (shields) of those with the armor, to help us protect those who were not ready for the battle.

A messenger came up to me, gave me a trumpet and told me to blow it quickly. I did, and those who had on at least some of their armor immediately responded, snapping to attention. More armor was brought to them, which they put on quickly. I noticed that those who had wounds did not put armor over their wounds, but before I could say anything about this enemy arrows began raining down on us. Everyone who did not have on all of his or her armor was wounded. Those who had not coveredtheirwoundswerestruckagainin thesameplace.

Those who were hit by arrows of slander immediately began to slander those who were not wounded. Those who were hit with gossip began to gossip, and soon a major division had been created within our camp. Then vultures swooped down to pick up the wounded to deliver them into the camp of prisoners. The wounded still had swords and could have smitten the vultures easily, but they didn't. They were actually carried off willingly because they were so angry at the rest of us.

The scene among those in the camp behind our army was even worse. There seemed to be total chaos. Thousands lay on the ground wounded and groaning. Many of those who were not wounded just sat in a stupor of unbelief. The wounded and those who sat in unbelief were being quickly carried away by the vultures. Some were trying to help the wounded, and keep the vultures off of them, but the wounded were so angry they would threaten and drive away those who were trying to help them.

"Immediately three great angels named Faith, Hope and Love came and stood behind us, and everyone's shield began to grow."

Many who were not wounded were simply running as fast as they could from the scene of battle. This first encounter with the enemy was so devastating that I was tempted to join them in their flight. Then, very quickly, some of these began reappearing with full suits of armor on, and large shields. The mirth of the party had changed into an awesome resolve. They began to take the places of those who had fallen, and even began forming new ranks to protect the rear and flanks. These brought great courage, and everyone resolved to stand and fight until death. Immediately three great angels named Faith, Hope and Love came and stood behind us, and everyone's shield began to grow.

The High-Way

We had swords named the Word of God, and arrows that were named for biblical truths. We wanted to shoot back, but did not know how to without hitting the Christians that were ridden by the demons. Then it occurred to us that if these Christians were hit with truth they would wake up and fight off their oppressors. I fired off a few arrows. Almost all of them hit Christians. However, when the arrow of truth went into them, they did not wake up, or fall down wounded—they became enraged, and the demon riding on them grew much larger. This shocked everyone, and we began to feel that this may be an impossible battle to win, but with Faith, Hope and Love we were very confident that we could at least hold our own ground. Another angel named Wisdom then appeared and directed us to fight from the mountain behind us.

On the mountain there were ledges at different levels for as high as you could see. At each higher level the ledges became narrower, and harder to stand on. Each level was named after a biblical truth. The lower levels were named after foundational truths such as "Salvation," "Sanctification," "Prayer," "Faith," etc., and the higher levels were named after more advanced biblical truths. The higher we climbed, the larger both our shields and our swords grew, and fewer of the enemy arrows could reach that position.

A Tragic Mistake

Some who had stayed on the lower levels began picking up the enemy arrows and shooting them back. This was a tragic mistake. The demons easily dodged the arrows and let them hit the Christians. When a Christian was hit by one of the arrows of Accusation or Slander, a demon of Bitterness or Rage would fly in and perch on that arrow. He would then begin to urinate and defecate his poison upon that Christian. When a Christian had two or three of these demons added to the Pride or Self-righteousness he already had, he began to change into the contorted image of the demons themselves.

We could see this happening from the higher levels, but those on the lower levels who were using the enemy's arrows could not see it. Half of us decided to keep climbing, while the other half descended back to the lower levels to explain to those still on them what was happening. Everyone was then warned to keep climbing and not stop, except for a few who stationed themselves on each level to keep the other soldiers moving higher.

Safety

When we reached the level called "The Unity of the Brethren," none of the enemy's arrows could reach us. Many in our camp decided that was as far as they needed to climb. I understood this because with each new level the footing was more precarious. However, I also felt much stronger and more skillful with my weapons the higher I went, so I continued climbing.

Soon my skills were good enough to shoot and hit the demons without hitting the Christians. I felt that if I kept going higher I could shoot far enough to hit the leaders of the evil horde who stayed behind their army. I was sorry that so many had stopped on the lower levels, where they were safe but could not hit the enemy. Even so, the strength and character that grew in those who kept climbing made them great champions, each of which I knew would destroy many of the enemy.

At each level there were arrows of Truth scattered about which I knew were left from those who had fallen from that position. All of the arrows were named after the Truth of that level. Some were reluctant to pick up these arrows, but I knew we needed all that we could to destroy the great horde below. I picked one up, shot it, and so easily hit a demon that the others started picking them up and shooting them. We began to decimate several of the enemy divisions. Because of this, the entire evil army focused its attention on us. For a time it seemed the more we achieved the more we were opposed. Though our task seemed endless, it had become exhilarating.

The Word Is Our Anchor

Our swords grew as we reached each level. I almost left mine behind because I did not seem to need it at the higher levels. I finally decided that it had been given to me for a purpose, so I had better keep it. I drove it into the ground and tied myself to it while I shot at the enemy. The voice of the Lord then came to me, saying: *"You have used the wisdom that will enable you to keep climbing. Many have fallen because they did not use their sword properly to anchor themselves."* No one else seemed to

hear this voice, but many saw what I had done and did the same thing.

I wondered why the Lord had not spoken to me before I had made this decision. I then had a sense of knowing that He had already spoken this to me somehow. Then I perceived that my whole life had been training for this hour. I was prepared to the degree that I had listened to the Lord and obeyed Him throughout my life. I also knew that for some reason the wisdom and understanding I now had could not be added to or taken away from while in this battle. I became profoundly thankful for every trial I had experienced in my life, and sorry for not appreciating them more at the time.

> *"I became profoundly thankful for every trial I had experienced in my life, and sorry for not appreciating them more at the time."*

Soon we were hitting the demons with almost perfect accuracy. Rage rose from the enemy army like fire and brimstone. I knew that the Christians trapped in that army were now feeling the brunt of that rage. Unable to hit us they were now shooting at each other. With his arrows now ineffective against us, the enemy sent the vultures to attack. Those who had not used their swords as anchors were able to strike down many of the vultures, but they too were being knocked from the ledges where they were standing. Some of these landed on a lower level, but some fell all the way to the bottom and were picked up and carried off by the vultures.

A New Weapon

The arrows of Truth would rarely penetrate the vultures, but they hurt them enough to drive them back. Every time they were driven back some of us would climb to the next level. When we reached the level called "Galatians Two Twenty," we were above the altitude that the vultures could fly. At this level the sky above almost blinded us with its brightness and beauty. I felt peace like I had never felt it before.

Previously much of my fighting spirit had really been motivated out of as much hatred and disgust for the enemy as it had been for the sake of the kingdom, truth, and love for the prisoners. But it was on this level that I caught up to Faith, Hope and Love, which before I had only been following at a distance. On this level I was almost overpowered by their glory. When I caught up to them they turned to me, and began repairing and shining my armor. Soon it was completely transformed and exuded the glory that was in them. When they touched my sword, great bolts of brilliant lightning began flashing from it. Love then said, "Those who reach this level are entrusted with the powers of the age to come, but I must teach you how to use them."

The "Galatians Two Twenty" level was so wide that there was no longer any danger of falling. There were also unlimited arrows with the name Hope written on them. We shot some of them down at the vultures, and these arrows killed them easily. About half who had reached this level kept shooting while the others began carrying these arrows down to those still on the lower levels.

The vultures kept coming in waves upon the levels below, but with each one there would be fewer than before. From "Galatians Two Twenty" we could hit any enemy in the army except the leaders themselves, who were still out of range. We decided not to use the arrows of Truth until we had destroyed all of the vultures, because the cloud of depression they created made the truth less effective. This took a very long time, but we never got tired.

Faith, Hope and Love, who had grown like our weapons with each level, were now so large that I knew people far beyond the battle area could see them. Their glory even radiated into the camp of prisoners who were still under a great cloud of vultures. The exhilaration continued to grow in all of us. I felt that being in this army, in this battle, had to be one of the greatest adventures of all time.

After destroying most of the vultures that had been attacking our mountain, we began picking off the vultures that had covered the prisoners. As the cloud of darkness began dissipating and the sun began to shine down on them, they began to wake up as if they had been in a deep sleep. They were immediately repulsed by their condition, especially by the vomit that still covered them, and began cleaning themselves up. As they beheld Faith, Hope and Love, they saw the mountain we were on and began running for it. The evil horde rained arrows of Accusation and Slander at them, but they did not stop. By the time they got to the mountain many had a dozen or more arrows stuck in them, but seemed not to even notice. As soon as they began to scale the mountain their wounds began to heal. With the cloud of depression being dispelled it seemed as if everything was getting much easier.

The Trap

The former prisoners had great joy in their salvation. They seemed so overwhelmed with appreciation for each level as they began to scale the mountain that it gave us a greater appreciation for those truths. Soon a fierce resolve to fight the enemy also arose in the former prisoners. They put on the armor provided and begged to be allowed to go back and attack the enemy. We thought about it, but then decided we should all stay on the mountain to fight. Again the voice of the Lord spoke, saying: *A second time you have chosen wisdom. You cannot win if you try to fight the enemy on his own ground, but must remain on My Holy mountain.*

I was stunned that we had made another decision of such importance by just thinking and discussing it briefly. I then resolved to do my best to not make another decision of any consequence without prayer. Wisdom then stepped up to me quickly, took both of my shoulders firmly and looked me intensely in the eyes, saying: *You must do this!* I then noticed that, even though I had been on the broad plateau of "Galatians Two Twenty," I had drifted to the very edge without even knowing it, and could have easily fallen. I looked again into the eyes of Wisdom, and he said with the utmost seriousness, *Take heed when you think you stand, lest you fall. In this life you can fall from any level.*

"The Lord Jesus Himself then stood in our midst."

The Serpents

For a long time we continued killing the vultures and picking off the demons that were riding the Christians. We found that the arrows of different Truths would have more of an impact on different demons. We knew that it was going to be a long battle, but we were not taking any more casualties now, and we had already passed the level of "Patience." Even so, after these Christians had the demons shot off of them, few would come to the mountain. Many had taken on the nature of the demons, and continued in their delusion without them. As the darkness of the demons dissipated we could see the ground moving around the feet of these Christians. Then I saw that their legs were bound by serpents called Shame.

We shot arrows of truth at the serpents, but they had little effect. We then tried the arrows of Hope, but without result. From "Galatians Two Twenty" it was very easy to go higher, so we started up to the higher levels. Soon we happened upon a garden that was the most beautiful place I had ever seen. Over the entrance to this garden was written, "The Father's Unconditional Love." It was the most glorious and inviting doorway I had ever seen, so we were compelled to enter. As soon as we did, we saw the Tree of Life in the middle of this garden. It was still guarded by angels of awesome strength. They looked as if they had been expecting us, so we had the courage to pass them and walk up to the tree. One of them said, *"Those who make it to this level, who know the Father's love, can eat."*

I did not realize how hungry I was. When I tasted the fruit, it was better than anything

I had ever tasted, but was also somehow familiar. It brought memories of sunshine, rain, beautiful fields, the sun setting over the ocean, but even more than that, of the people I loved. With every bite I loved everything and everyone more. Then my enemies started coming to mind, and I loved them, too. The feeling was soon greater than anything I had ever experienced, even the peace on "Galatians Two Twenty." Then I heard the voice of the Lord, and He said, *"This is now your daily bread. It shall never be withheld from you. You may eat as much and as often as you like. There is no end to My love."*

I looked up into the tree to see where the voice had come from, and saw that it was filled with pure white eagles. They had the most beautiful, penetrating eyes I have ever seen. They were looking at me as if waiting for instructions. One of the angels said, "They will do your bidding. These eagles eat snakes." I said, *"Go! Devour the shame that has bound our brothers."* They opened their wings and a great wind came that lifted them into the air. These eagles filled the sky with a blinding glory. Even as high as we were, I could hear the sounds of terror from the enemy camp at the sight of these eagles coming toward them.

The Lord Jesus Himself then stood in our midst. He touched each one, then said, *"I must now share with you what I shared with your brothers after My ascension—the message of My kingdom. The enemy's most powerful army has now been put to flight, but not destroyed. Now it is time for us to march forth with the gospel of My kingdom. The eagles have been released and will go with us. We will take arrows from every level, but I am your Sword, and I am your Captain. It is now time for the Sword of the Lord to be unsheathed."*

I then turned and saw that the entire army of the Lord was standing in that garden. There were men women and children from all races and nations, each carrying their banners that moved in the wind with perfect unity. I knew that nothing like this had been seen in the earth before. I knew that the enemy had many more armies, and fortresses throughout the earth, but none could stand before this great army. I said almost under my breath, "This must be the day of the Lord." The whole host then answered in an awesome thunder, "The day of the Lord of Hosts has come." ■

Mustard Seeds of Wisdom

"For we do not wrestle against flesh and blood, but against principalities, against powers, against the rulers of the darkness of this age, against spiritual hosts of wickedness in the heavenly places. Therefore, take up the whole armor of God that you may be able to withstand in the evil day, and having done all, to stand."

— Ephesians 6:12-13 (NKJV)

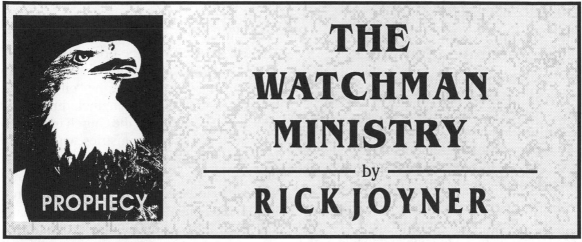

THE WATCHMAN MINISTRY
by
RICK JOYNER

PROPHECY

All Scriptures NAS unless otherwise noted.

It is a basic aspect of the prophetic ministry to be a "watchman." Prophets in the Old Testament are often called watchmen because this was a significant characteristic of their ministry, as we see in Ezekiel 3:17. With the prophetic ministry now being restored to its proper place in the body of Christ, this aspect of the ministry is becoming increasingly important for us to understand if we are to function in it productively.

The prophet was called a watchman because he basically functioned in the spiritual realm just as the literal watchmen did in the natural realm. The natural watchmen were stationed at specific posts on the walls of the city that gave them the visibility to watch for the king or other members of the nobility to announce their coming. They were also to look for enemies from without, or disorder arising within the city, or camp of Israel.

These watchmen were especially trained to be able to distinguish the enemy from their brethren. Only those with the best vision and judgment were given these posts. They could not be overly prone to sound the alarm, or to request that the gates be opened. They had to be accurate in their discernment. If there were too many false alarms the people would begin to disregard them. If they were careless and let an enemy in the gate, they could jeopardize the entire city. This was an extremely crucial position for which accuracy and dependability were required.

Each ministry given to the church can only function properly if it is correctly related to the other ministries. Because all ministries are still being restored to their true biblical place, the watchman ministry cannot function properly until the other ministries have taken their proper place. However, until that time comes, we must do what we can in the place to which we have been appointed, helping to bring clarity of function to the other ministries.

There are many today who consider themselves watchmen who are obviously not called to that ministry. In some cases these people are making a noble attempt to fill a void left by those who have been called as watchmen but have not taken their place. Even so, the misuse of this title has resulted in confusion regarding this ministry, and the rejection of it altogether by many who see it being used improperly. The answer is not to reject this ministry, but to pursue the precise functioning of it by those who have been called as watchmen. This will become an increasingly critical ministry as we proceed toward the end of this age.

The Watchmen Stations

The biblical positions of the watchmen were, 1) on the walls of the city (see Isaiah 62:6-7); 2) walking about in the city (see Song of Solomon 3:3); and 3) "on the hills," or country-side (see Jeremiah 31:6). Viewed together these provide us with a practical picture of the operation of this ministry.

Being on the walls of the city would place one in a position of elevated perspective to see both a distance outside and inside of the city. These were trained to recognize both the enemy and their brethren from a great distance. However, they had no authority to confront either. They simply gave their information to the elders who sat in the gates. Only the elders had the authority to either command that the gates be opened or to sound the alarm.

The watchmen appointed to walk about inside the city could more closely observe activity within. These were specifically trained to make a way for the king or the nobility who were passing, or to recognize and confront disorder or unlawful behavior from their brethren. They could apprehend violators, but they could not imprison them or impose sentences. This was the duty of the elders who served as judges.

The watchmen "on the hills," patrolled the borders and countryside. They could see both the enemy or the nobility long before they got to the cities. They, too, were specially trained to distinguish their countrymen from their enemies, or from foreigners who came as traders or ambassadors. Again, they did not have the authority to call for a mobilization of the defenses, or to let foreigners freely pass, but they communicated what they saw to the elders who did have that authority.

In Revelation 21:2 the bride of the Lamb is referred to as a city. Therefore relating to the position of watchmen, the "city" would be indicative of the church, including either a local congregation or the church universal. The Lord has called ministries whose main function is to be such watchmen in each of these three places. He has some whose only purpose is to be watching within the church for the movement of the King, and to make a way for Him. They are also called to recognize and report disorder, or unlawful behavior to the elders. There are some who have been given such a place of vision that they can see both inside and outside of the church. There are also watchmen whose main calling is to roam around as scouts in the world. They might see cults rising, or detect a major persecution before it breaks out against the church.

Watching and Praying

In Isaiah 62:6-7 the function of the watchman was both to pray and to guard. This is crucial because most of our discernment will come through prayer. In Ezekiel 3:17 the watchman was to hear from the Lord and warn the people. This is where many who are called as watchmen depart from their course. They begin looking for the enemy more than they listen to the Lord, and both their vision and discernment becomes distorted.

The watchman ministry is spiritual. True spiritual vision is in the spiritual realm, which is entered through prayer and worship. Prayer helps to purify our vision. The prayers of the watchmen can sometimes quiet the disorder or drive away the enemy without even having to notify the elders or sound the alarm. The first principle of this ministry is that more than looking for the enemy, the watchman must be in communication with the Lord. Jeremiah 6:17, Isaiah 21:5-10 and Habakkuk 2:1-3 address this aspect of the watchman ministry.

Knowing the Times

One of the basic functions of this ministry, which is often overlooked but is desperately needed, is *knowing the times* (Isaiah 21:11-12). You can probably remember an old movie where the watchman walks about the city and calls out, "Twelve o'clock and all's well." I have met many people with prophetic gifts, but only a couple who could accurately foretell both the events and *their timing*. As we proceed toward the end of this age, timing will become increasingly critical in all that we do. We must pray for the Lord to raise up the last day **"sons of Issachar, men who understood the times, with knowledge of what Israel should do" (I Chronicles 12:32).**

One of the psalmist's most desperate lamentations for his nation under siege was: **"We do not see our signs; there is no longer any prophet, nor is there any among us who knows how long" (Psalm 74:9).** The Lord wants His people to know *when* He is going to move, *when* judgment is coming, and *when* the enemy will come. This is an *essential* aspect of the prophetic ministry that must be recovered and positioned correctly in the body or we will continue to pay with unnecessary defeats and catastrophes. We would do well to ask the same question that Job asked:

> **Why are times ["of judgment," margin] not stored up by the Almighty, and why do those who know Him not see His days [timing]?**
> **Some remove the landmarks; they seize and devour flocks (Job 24:1-2).**

If you read the rest of the chapter it is almost a commentary on the present condition of much of the body of Christ. When we fail to recognize the timing of the Lord, even our spiritual boundaries become blurred. We simply must have this ministry, with its discernment fully operational, restored to its proper place in the church.

The Proper Sphere of Authority

The watchmen were not the elders in the gates, nor did they have the authority to open or close the gates of a city. Neither did they have the authority to mobilize the militia against the enemy. Their job was to communicate what they saw to those who did have the authority. Presently, many pastors and elders are trying to do this job for their congregations, which only distracts them from their true calling. We must begin to recognize, train, and position those who have this calling, and establish effective lines of communication with them.

It is understandable that many leaders are either wary or weary of those who claim to be watchmen. Many who claim this position are just fearful or suspicious people who presume an office to which they have not been called. Many others who do have the calling try to use their gifts to usurp the authority of the elders in order to dictate policy or actions. Trust is the bridge that makes relationships possible. You can have genuine forgiveness and love, but there can be no real relationship without trust. Until trust is established between the elders and the watchmen, they will not be able to function together as God intends.

Many leaders are so wounded and weary from the ministries of those who presumed to be watchmen or prophets that they do not want anything to do with this ministry today. Likewise, many watchmen have been so wounded by pastors that they have lost their trust in the leadership of the church. There is usually a lot to overcome on both sides, but those who are true on both sides will overcome this barrier. We have no choice if we are going to walk in the unity that both the Lord and the times we live in require. It will not be easy for either side to rebuild the bridge of trust, but it will be worth it.

The pastors and elders will never be able to function on the level of authority they are called to until the watchmen take the burdens off of them that they themselves have been called to carry. But let us understand that the required trust on both sides is something that only comes with faithfulness—we must never give up on each other. Every relationship is tested. The greater the tests that we endure, the stronger the relationship will ultimately be. Until a scriptural relationship between leaders and watchmen is established, the watchmen cannot function, and the leaders will continue to be needlessly blind-sided by the enemy.

Paul talked about how careful he was to stay within the realm of authority that had been appointed to him (see II Corinthians 10:12-14). He knew that if he got outside of the limits that God had set for him he would be vulnerable to the enemy, or worse. Leaders must learn to let the watchmen do what they are called to do, and watchmen must learn that it is their job to simply transmit information—not to dictate policy. When our burden is transferred to the next realm of authority it is no longer our burden, and we will be transgressing if we try to keep it.

Likewise, a watchman who is appointed to patrol out in the world (researching cults, political or philosophical trends, etc.) will become a stumbling block if he also tries to watch over what is going on inside the church. Similarly, those who are given to watch over the church can develop an unhealthy paranoia when they start trying to see what is going on out in the world. It is hard for watchmen to stay within their realm of authority, and when they do not, the consequences will almost always be destructive.

Interpreting Revelations

One of the biggest areas of failure in the prophetic ministry, including in those who serve as watchmen, is in the area of interpreting revelations such as dreams and visions. This is usually caused by a tendency to allow personal factors to influence interpretations. I have observed that the following twelve factors are most often responsible for these failures.

1   Presumption

Many of those who function in what we call watchman ministries are self-appointed, or prematurely appointed, and are not skilled in the use of the gift of discernment that is required for this ministry. These usually substitute suspicion for true discernment. This is rooted in fear, which will *always* distort our perception. True discernment can only operate in true, godly love. "God is love," and if we are going to see with His eyes we must see through the eyes of love. Neither is God afraid of the enemy, and anything that is colored by fear is a distortion of true spiritual vision.

2   Majoring on Minors

The first calling of the watchman is to prepare the way for the King, not to look for the enemy. When we are primarily focused on looking for the enemy a very serious distortion of our vision takes place. How many so-called "watchman ministries" have ever foreseen the Lord coming in a new movement, and begun to prepare the way for Him? I have not witnessed a single case of this, which should tell us something about the true character of that ministry. Those who are always looking for the enemy instead of the Lord will be in jeopardy of becoming the "fault-finders" that Jude wrote about, doing more damage to the church themselves than many enemy attacks.

The Lord commended the church of Thyatira for *not* knowing the deep things of Satan (see Revelation 2:24). We will be changed into the image of what we are beholding (see II Corinthians 3:18). If we are beholding the glory of the Lord we will be changed into His image. If we are spending too much time looking for or at the enemy, we will be changed into his image, and be used as an accuser of the brethren. This is why many of the heresy hunters become so mean-spirited, and easily depart from biblical teachings on bringing correction in the church while they claim to be protectors of the Scripture. We must be vigilant and able to quickly recognize the enemy, but not be too quick to call someone the enemy until we are sure of what we see. It is not wise to trust the vision of anyone who does not see the Lord and what He is doing much more than they see the enemy.

3  Prejudices

These can be cultural or religious. If we are prone to be prejudiced toward a race, sex, age group, denomination or movement, it can seriously distort what we are seeing. Jesus came to save the whole world, and in Christ **"There is neither Jew nor Greek, there is neither slave nor free man, there is neither male nor female; for you are all one in Christ Jesus"** (Galatians 3:28). Prejudice against any such group is a serious spiritual flaw that the enemy will exploit.

4  Doctrines

The Lord does not give prophecies to verify doctrines—He gave the Bible for that. Those who use prophecy to establish doctrines usually evolve into a cult. It is a characteristic of the prophetic ministry to exhort the people to either maintain, or return to, the established precepts of the faith, but never to establish them. Those who have a "pet doctrine" they are trying to promote, or an agenda to convince others of a doctrinal emphasis other than Christ Jesus Himself, should not be trusted in a watchman's position.

It has been the downfall of many anointed prophetic men and women to try to become teachers. There are some who are called as prophets *and* teachers, but they are usually those who are being prepared for an apostolic commission. When one who is called as a prophet tries to be a teacher, or when one who is called as a teacher tries to be a prophet, the consequences have been devastating.

5 Rejection

Prophets are often rejected, but must never let rejection grip their spirit. The Lord often allows His prophets to be rejected to deliver them from the fear of man. If we are overly affected by rejection we are still not delivered, and will always be in jeopardy of compromising the ministry. Rejection keeps us self-centered instead of Christ-centered, which causes a distortion in our vision. Rejection, if not healed, usually turns into bitterness.

6 Bitterness and Resentment

The priests in the Old Testament could not have boils. Boils are little unhealed wounds that have become infected. One who has boils is overly sensitive and hard to touch. When spiritual wounds are not healed and become infected they turn into bitterness, and a root of bitterness can defile many.

The only difference between a spiritual sheep dog that protects the sheep, and a wolf that devours them, is that the wolf has unhealed wounds. Most false prophets were called as true prophets of the Lord. Many of the grumblers and faultfinders that Jude warned the church about are gifted prophets and watchmen who have become bitter and critical. Forgiving is basic Christianity, and whenever we fail to forgive we are departing from the path of life.

7  Rebellion

Rebellion is usually rooted in either rejection or self-will, both of which can be deadly to the prophetic ministry. Extreme rebellion is usually evidenced by the declaration that we will not be submitted to men, but only to God. This is an inverted perversion of the most deadly kind of the fear of man. Since God usually speaks and works through men, such a mentality is in profound delusion. The true fear of God, which is not subject to the fear of man, is free to properly recognize, honor and submit to all who are anointed by God. There can be a fine line between revelation and divination. Because **"rebellion is as the sin of divination [witchcraft], and insubordination is as iniquity and idolatry" (I Samuel 15:23)**, we must be diligent to guard our hearts against rebellion or insubordination. This can be the biggest open door for the enemy to enter our own ministry, as in King Saul's case.

8  Unsanctified Mercy

This is having mercy for the things that God is judging. Intercessors often take on the burdens of the people, but prophets must carry the burden of God. Very often these are in conflict. It was for this reason that Peter received one of the biggest rebukes in Scripture: **"Get behind Me Satan! You are a stumbling block to Me; *for you are not setting your mind on God's interests, but man's"* (Matthew 16:23).** Jesus never responded to human need, but only to what He saw the Father doing. He had compassion for human needs, but compassion did not dictate His actions. The Father alone did.

Those who are ruled by human compassion instead of by the Holy Spirit will often be used by the enemy in one of his primary strategies for wearing down the saints—infiltrating the church with "false brethren." These are not false prophets or teachers, but false Christians. They are sent to steal the children's bread by consuming the leadership's time and ministry, while producing little fruit of change.

9  The "Party Spirit"

When we derive our recognition from a single organization, there will almost always be pressure to prophesy the "party line." This makes it very difficult not to compromise prophetic integrity. All true authority for ministry comes from the Lord, not the church, and certainly not just a segment of the church. Ordination papers are the equivalent of letters of recommendation that were used by the first century church, and are helpful for verifying ministries. It is also proper that we should be submitted to a local church, and sometimes a movement of churches. But we must always understand that true authority comes from above. If we are to represent the Lord properly to those that we serve, we must guard against, and sometimes stand against this party spirit. Unchecked it will pervert prophetic integrity, and the church or movement that we have been given to help watch for. The high priest carried the stones of all of the tribes on his heart (in the breastplate), and if we are to walk in the high calling we must always carry the whole church on our heart, not just one tribe.

10 Failing to Submit to the Body

This can be caused by rebellion, rejection or just plain negligence, and it will be costly. It is rare to even find someone who can interpret their own dreams and visions. Even those I know to be especially gifted in interpreting the dreams or visions of others are usually incapable of interpreting accurately what God has given to them. The Lord limits us in this way because He wants us all to need each other, which should ultimately lead to our loving each other. The prophetic people that I know who consistently hear from the Lord on the highest levels, rarely hear from the Lord about important matters concerning their own lives. Instead, they are dependent on others to give them a word when they need it.

Every true minister I know, including the greatest prophets, has a major blind spot in their life which makes them dependent on others to see for them. If we do not learn to work together and trust each other's special gifts, we will be hit by the enemy in those blind spots. This is especially true of the last day prophetic ministry, which must function in unity as Isaiah declared: **"Your watchmen shall lift up their voices, with their voices they shall sing *together*; for *they shall see eye to eye* [together] when the LORD brings back Zion" (Isaiah 52:8 NKJV).**

11 Lust

In Isaiah 29:10 prophets are referred to as "eyes." The function of the prophet is to be the eyes of the body. As the Lord explained, **"The light of the body is the eye: therefore when thine eye is *single*, thy whole body also is full of light (Luke 11:34 KJV)."** This speaks of the unity as discussed above, but it also speaks of the fact that if we are going to use our eyes for the Lord, we must use them only for Him, if we expect to be "full of light."

Job declared, **"I have made a covenant with my eyes; how then could I gaze at a virgin?" (Job 31:1).** Job made a covenant with his eyes not to look upon that which would cause him to stumble. If we desire prophetic vision we would do well to make that same covenant, that our eyes belong to the Lord and we will not use them for evil. Lust is one of the primary destroyers of prophetic vision. Lust is ultimate, basic selfishness, the exact opposite of the nature of the Lord, as well as the nature of the true prophetic ministry.

12 Our Natural Eyes versus "the Eyes of Our Heart"

In Ephesians 1:18-19 Paul prayed that the "eyes of our hearts" would be open. These are our spiritual eyes, which see the realm of the spirit more clearly than our natural eyes see the natural realm. This comes with experience and maturity, but if we are to be prophetic we must see into the realm of the spirit. Otherwise, we will be judging by our natural perception, which very often will be amiss.

Being prophetic is much more than being perceptive in the natural. Occasionally the Lord may anoint a perception in the natural and use it for revelation, but more often than not, *natural appearances will lead to wrong conclusions.* This even happened to the great prophet Samuel who did not have any of his words fall to the ground, but received this rebuke from the Lord:

> **Do not look at his appearance or at the height of his stature, because I have rejected him; for God sees not as man sees, for man looks at the outward appearance, but the LORD looks at the heart (I Samuel 16:7).**

God does not see as man sees, and if we are going to be used as His eye for the body, we must learn this lesson well.

Summary

The Lord is restoring the prophetic ministry to the full biblical stature to which it was appointed. Even so, we must recognize that, in general, its proper connection to the rest of the body and the other equipping ministries given to the church has not yet been made functional. To a large degree this has been the result of failures on the part of the present leadership of the church, as well as those emerging with true prophetic gifts. This is to be expected, but it also must be overcome.

One of the primary functions of the emerging prophetic ministry is to serve as spiritual watchman for the church. This will be on all levels, some being assigned to local congregations and ministries, and some serving more on a national or international level. As these watchman ministries become more accurate and dependable, we will seldom be needlessly blindsided by the enemy again. We can be prepared for his assaults and turn them back. Sometimes we will even be able to start setting ambushes for him. This alone will make a major difference in the effectiveness of the entire church.

As watchmen become effective in taking the burden off the leadership of the church, the leadership will do what they have been called to do. Great spiritual advances will result. However, if we are called to this watchman ministry, let us be patient in waiting for our placement. If we have a true gift, and manifest the fruit of the Spirit, our gift will make a place for us. Our goal must always be first to gain the endorsement of God, not men. If we want the endorsement of God we must be devoted to truth, integrity, and submission to His Spirit. If it takes others a while to acknowledge our calling, while we are waiting we can grow in grace and discernment. **"For if the bugle produces an indistinct sound, who will prepare himself for battle?" (I Corinthians 14:8).** When you can produce a distinct sound, the church will hear you.

We must also understand that the watchman ministry was not given to bring correction to the church—the elders were given for that purpose. Watchmen are called to give accurate information to the elders and then trust and support what they do with that information. The Old Covenant prophetic ministry was often devoted to bringing correction, but usually the correction was given to the kings or elders. However, we do not see the New Covenant prophet being used nearly as much in that way because this duty was assumed more by the apostles and elders.

If we are called to bring correction, we must follow the biblical procedures such as those outlined in Matthew 18. If the Lord does show us something that is wrong with someone, our first response must be to go to that person in private. If He shows us something that is wrong in a congregation, we must take it in private to those who have been appointed to lead that congregation. I have never heard a word of correction given openly in an assembly that I thought was from the Lord. In fact, I have witnessed several tragic mistakes made this way.

The Lord used a word of knowledge to bring correction to the woman at the well. We would do well to learn from the great wisdom and gentleness with which He did this.

continued on page 94

A COUNTRY LAD BECOMES A WORLD POWER

by

ARTHUR PERCY FITT

All Scriptures KJV unless otherwise noted.

Sam P. Jones, the great Georgia evangelist of over a generation ago, was once attacked by a newspaper man who said that the papers had made him. Sam replied, with his characteristic drawl, "Then let them make another."

Starting from nothing, D. L. Moody (1837-1899) became one of the most influential spiritual figures that America has ever produced. What could account for his rise? It is sometimes said that Northfield, Massachusetts made D. L. Moody, meaning his sturdy ancestry and the rugged life of New England. While granting certain values to heredity and environment we can still ask, "If so, why has not Northfield produced another D. L. Moody?" The secret of his power and influential career must be found in quite other sources.

Biologists might claim that Mr. Moody was an accidental deviation from the normal conditions and antecedents into which he was born, like Benjamin Franklin, amazingly unique among thirteen children. I agree he was a unique phenomenon, but that would be to judge on a merely materialistic plane, ignoring important factors in his life. I would rather list him with a few outstanding men in church history like John Wesley, Martin Luther, and with men of the Bible like Paul, John the Baptist and Moses. In each of these lives there were spiritual crises, and each received vision and enduement from God for special work appropriate to their special time and need.

Four decisive events in Moody's life, major crises, account step by step for his rise. They are, chronologically:

1. His acceptance of Jesus of Nazareth as his Savior, in Boston as a lad of 18 in 1855;

2. His first impressive experience in soul-winning in Chicago in 1860, aged 23;

3. His first realization of the immeasurable fullness of the Bible in Chicago in 1867;

4. His filling with the Holy Spirit in New York in 1872.

He became a believer in Jesus Christ under his Sunday school teacher's leading in

Boston. He got a taste of soul-winning by observing a dying teacher of his Sunday school in Chicago. He became a man of the Bible under the ministry of Harry Moorehouse, an English evangelist and Bible teacher. His Pentecostal experience made him a soul-winning evangelist to nations.

How He Came to Believe in Jesus

Young Moody left home early in 1854, and after a time found a job with two uncles in their shoe store in Boston. Among conditions they imposed on the boy was attendance at Mount Vernon Congregational Church and Sunday school. It was a revival church, with a zealous and eloquent minister, Dr. Edward Norris Kirk, but it was in connection with the Sunday school that he found God. Here he was assigned to a young men's class taught by one Edward Kimball. He knew little about the Bible or its teachings, but he gave close, respectful attention to his teacher, and his demeanor in class was always earnest. Let Mr. Kimball take up the story:

I determined to speak to him about Christ and about his soul, and started down to Holton's shoe store. When I was nearly there I began to wonder whether I ought to go in just then during business hours. I thought that possibly my call might embarrass the boy, and that when I went away the other clerks would ask who I was, and taunt him with my efforts in trying to make him a good boy. In the meantime I had passed the store, and discovering this I determined to make a dash for it and have it done with.

I found Moody in the back part of the building wrapping up shoes. I went up to him at once, and putting my hand on his shoulder I made what I afterwards felt was a very weak plea for Christ. I don't know just what words I used, nor could Mr. Moody tell. I simply told him of Christ's love for him and the love Christ wanted in return. That was all there was. It seemed the young man was just ready for the light that then broke upon him, and there, in the back of that store in Boston, he gave himself and his life to Christ.

How tenderly he used to refer to that unforgettable transaction between himself and his Savior! I heard him preaching in Tremont Temple, in 1897, when he said:

I can almost throw a stone from Tremont Temple to the spot where I found God over forty years ago. I wish I could do something to lead some young man to the same God. I wish I could make people understand what He has been to me. He has been a million times better to me than I have been to Him.

At another time he said:

The morning I was converted I went outdoors and fell in love with everything. I never loved the bright sun shining over the earth so much before, and when I heard the birds singing their sweet songs I fell in love with the birds. Everything was different.

Mr. Moody did not often refer to his conversion. But then he was reticent in speaking about other great experiences in his own life, and about his evangelistic campaigns. He did not live on the past. He seemed to face forward toward coming opportunities in full assurance of faith.

He took me to see that shoe store, 43 Court Street, in 1897. A marker was placed on the building in 1930. Since then the building has been torn down and a new building erected, on which a worthy bronze marker will identify the site in coming years.

How He Became a Soul-winner

Mr. Moody was led to give up flattering business prospects in Chicago in 1860 through a heart-searching experience of soul-winning which he witnessed and shared in. The story can be told in his own words, quoting from my book, *Shorter Life:*

> I had never lost sight of Jesus Christ since the first time I met Him in the store at Boston, but for years I really believed that I could not work for God. No one had ever asked me to do anything.

> When I went to Chicago I hired four pews in a church, as was the custom, and used to go out on the street and pick up young men and fill these pews. I never spoke to those young men about their souls: that was the work of the elders, I thought. After working for some time like that, I started a mission Sabbath school. I thought numbers were everything, and so I worked for numbers. When the attendance ran below one thousand it troubled me, and when it ran to twelve or fifteen hundred I was elated. Still none were converted, there was no harvest.

> Then God opened my eyes. There was a class of young ladies in the school who were without exception the most frivolous set of girls I ever met. One Sunday the teacher was ill, and I took that class. They laughed in my face, and I felt like opening the door and telling them all to get out and never come back.

> That week the teacher of the class came into the store where I worked. He was pale, and looked ill.

> "What is the trouble?" I asked.

> "I have had another hemorrhage of my lungs. The doctor says I cannot live on Lake Michigan, so I am going to New York State. I suppose I am going home to die."

> He seemed greatly troubled, and when I asked the reason he replied:

> "Well, I have never led any of my class to Christ. I really believe I have done the girls more harm than good."

> I had never heard any one talk like that before, and it set me thinking. After awhile I said:

> "Suppose you go and tell them how you feel! I will go with you in a carriage, if you want to go."

> He consented, and we started out together. It was one of the best journeys I ever had on earth. We went to the house of one of the girls, called for her, and the teacher talked to her about her soul. There was no laughing then! Tears stood in her eyes before long. After he had explained

the way of life he suggested that we have prayer. He asked me to pray. True, I had never done such a thing in my life as to pray God to convert a young lady there and then. But we prayed, and God answered our prayer.

We went to other houses. He would go upstairs, and be all out of breath, and he would tell the girls what he had come for. It wasn't long before they broke down and sought salvation.

When his strength gave out I took him back to his lodgings. The next day we went out again. At the end of ten days he came to the store with his face literally shining.

"Mr. Moody," he said, "the last one of my class has yielded herself to Christ!"

I tell you we had a time of rejoicing.

He had to leave the next night, so I called his class together that night for a prayer meeting, and there God kindled a fire in my soul that has never gone out. The height of my ambition had been to be a successful merchant, and if I had known that meeting was going to take that ambition out of me I might not have gone. But how many times I have thanked God since for that meeting! The dying teacher sat in the midst of his class, and talked with them, and read the 14th chapter of John. We tried to sing "Blest be the Tie That Binds," after which we knelt down to pray. I was just rising from my knees when one of the class began to pray for her dying teacher. Another prayed, and another, and before we rose the whole class had prayed. As I went out I said to myself: "O God, let me die rather than lose the blessing I have received tonight!"

The next evening I went to the depot to say good-bye to that teacher. Just before the train started, one of the class came, and before long, without any prearrangement they were all there. What a meeting that was! We tried to sing, but we broke down. The last we saw of that dying teacher he was standing on the platform of the rear car, his finger pointing upward, telling us to meet him in heaven.

I didn't know what this was going to cost me. I was disqualified for business: it had become distasteful to me. I had got a taste of another world, and cared no more for making money. For some days after the greatest struggle of my life took place. Should I give up business and give myself wholly to Christian work, or should I not? God helped me to decide aright, and I have never regretted my choice. Oh, the luxury of leading someone out of the darkness of this world into the glorious light and liberty of the gospel!

D. L. Moody gave up business for personal profit once and for all, and never afterward tried to accumulate wealth.

How He Became a Man of the Bible

The next great crisis in Mr. Moody's career occurred when he came to realize the immeasurable fullness of the Bible. The story is most suggestive. It begins early in 1867, when the doctor advised a sea voyage for Mrs. Moody, who had a harassing cough. They decided to go to England for two reasons: Mrs. Moody was born in London and a sister was still living there, and Mr. Moody wanted to hear and meet some of the great Christian leaders in England, such as Charles Haddon Spurgeon of London, George Williams, founder of the Y.M.C.A., and George Mueller of Bristol.

In the course of that trip Mr. Moody also went to Dublin, where he met Harry Moorehouse, "the boy preacher," who introduced himself and said he would like to come to Chicago and preach. This incident had an important sequel which can be told in Mr. Moody's own words, again quoting from my *Shorter Life:*

I looked at him. He was a beardless boy; didn't look as if he was more than seventeen; and I said to myself, "He can't preach!" He wanted me to let him know what boat I was going on as he would like to return with me. I thought he could not preach, and did not let him know. But I had not been in Chicago a great many weeks before I got a letter which said he had arrived in this country, and that he would come to Chicago and preach for me if I wanted him. I sat down and wrote a very cold letter: "If you come West, call on me." I thought that would be the last I should hear of him, but soon I got another letter, saying that he was still in this country and would come on if I wanted him. I wrote again, telling him if he happened to come West to drop in on me. In the course of a few days I got a letter stating that next Thursday he would be in Chicago. What to do with him I did not know. I had made up my mind he couldn't preach. I was going to be out of town Thursday and Friday, and I told some of the officers of the church:

"There is a man coming here Thursday who wants to preach. I don't know whether he can or not. You had better let him try, and I will be back Saturday."

They said there was a good deal of interest in the church, and they did not think they should have him preach then; he was a stranger, and he might do more harm than good.

"Well," I said, "you had better try him. Let him preach two nights," and they finally let him preach.

When I got back Saturday morning I was anxious to know how he got on. The first thing I said to my wife when I got in the house was:

"How is that young Irishman coming along?" (I had met him in Dublin and took him to be an Irishman, but he happened to be an Englishman.) "How do the people like him?"

"They like him very much."

"Did you hear him?"

"Yes."

"Did you like him?"

"Yes, very much. He has preached two sermons from John 3:16, '**For God so loved the world, that he gave his only begotten Son, that whosoever believeth in him should**

not perish, but have everlasting life'; and I think you will like him, although he preaches a little different from what you do."

"How is that?"

"Well, he tells sinners God loves them."

"Well," said I, "he is wrong."

She said: "I think you will agree with him when you hear him because he backs up everything he says with the Word of God."

I went down to church that night, and I noticed every one brought his Bible.

"My friends," began Moorehouse, "if you will turn to the third chapter of John and the sixteenth verse, you will find my text."

He preached a most extraordinary sermon from that verse. He did not divide the text into "Secondly" and "Thirdly" and "Fourthly." He just took it as a whole, and then went through the Bible from Genesis to Revelation to prove that in all ages God loved the world; that He sent prophets and patriarchs and holy men to warn them, and last of all sent His Son. After they murdered Him, He sent the Holy Ghost.

I never knew up to that time that God loved us so much. This heart of mine began to thaw out, and I could not keep back the tears. It was like news from a far country. I just drank it in.

The next night there was a great crowd, for the people like to hear that God loves them, and he said, "My friends, if you will turn in your Bible to the third chapter of John and the sixteenth verse you will find my text!" He preached another extraordinary sermon from that wonderful verse, and he went on proving God's love again from Genesis to Revelation. He could turn to almost any part of the Bible and prove it. I thought that sermon was better than the other one. He struck a higher chord than ever, and it was sweet to my soul to hear it.

The next night was Monday, and it is pretty hard to get out a crowd in Chicago on Monday night, but they came. Women left their washing, or if they washed they came and brought their Bibles. He said again, "My friends, if you will turn to the sixteenth verse of the third chapter of John you will find my text," and again he followed it out to prove that God loves us. He just beat it down into our hearts, and I have never doubted it since.

I used to preach that God was behind the sinner with a double-edged sword, ready to hew him down. I have got done with that. I preach now that God is behind the sinner with love, and he is running away from the God of love.

Tuesday night came, and we thought surely he had exhausted that text and would take another, but he preached the sixth sermon from that wonderful text, **"God so loved the world, that he gave his only begotten Son,** that whosoever believeth in Him should not perish, but have [not going to have when you die, but have it right here, now] everlasting life." Although many years have rolled away his hearers never have forgotten it.

The seventh night came, and he went into the pulpit. Every eye was upon him. All were anxious to know what he was going to preach about. He said, "My friends, I have been hunting all day for a new text, but I cannot find one as good as the old one, so we will go back to the third chapter of John and the sixteenth verse," and he preached the seventh sermon from that wonderful text. I remember the closing of that sermon. Said he:

"My friends, for a whole week I have been trying to tell you how much God loves you, but I cannot do it with this poor stammering tongue. If I could borrow Jacob's ladder, and climb up into heaven and ask Gabriel, who stands in the presence of the Almighty, if he could tell me how much love the Father has for the world, all he could say would be, **'God so loved the world, that he gave his only begotten Son, that whosoever believeth in him should not perish, but have everlasting life.' "**

It was a revelation to Mr. Moody of the inexhaustibility of Scripture such as he had never dreamed of. From that time he became a more diligent student of the Bible. He asked Moorehouse how to study, and invited friends to his Chicago home for probably the first "Bible readings" ever held in America.

How He Was Filled with the Holy Spirit

It is difficult to give an accurate account of the next outstanding crisis in Mr. Moody's life. We are face to face with divine mystery, but yet reality. Mr. Moody told the story of it several times during the seven years I was with him, but never in close detail, and I think his words were never reported in full. He regarded it as almost too solemn to talk about in public, but sometimes when he was speaking on God the Holy Spirit, he would testify to his own overpowering experience.

Let us begin in Chicago in the 1860s, after a church was organized out of his Sunday school converts and their families. Illinois Street Church was the scene of continuous revival activity, with Mr. Moody as its moving spirit, and frequently the preacher. Two faithful and devout women used to attend his meetings and sit on the front seat. He could see by the expression on their faces that they were praying, and at the close of the service they would tell him they were praying for him. They sensed something lacking.

Praying for him! Why? What for? Wasn't he full of zeal and activity for God? Why didn't they pray for the people?

"We are praying for you that you may receive the power."

"Haven't I got the power?"

"No, we are praying for you because you need the power of the Holy Spirit."

"I need the power! Why," said Mr. Moody, speaking of it in after years,

"I thought I had power. I had the largest congregations in Chicago, and there were many conversions. I was in a sense satisfied. But right along those godly women kept praying for me, and their earnest talk about anointing for special service set me to thinking. I asked them to come and talk with me, and we got down on our knees. They poured out their hearts that I might receive the filling of the Holy Spirit. There came a great hunger into my soul. I did not know what it was. I began to cry as I never did before. The hunger increased. I really felt that I did not want to live any longer if I could not have this power for service."

Chicago was laid in ashes while he was in this mental and spiritual condition. The Great Fire commenced on October 8, 1871, and swept out of existence the whole north section of the city where he lived and worked. His church was burnt and his flock scattered. Under these circumstances he left for the East to raise money for relief and the wherewithal to build a new church.

Mr. Douglas Russell, an English evangelist, supplies a link here. He says he was holding meetings in New York early in 1872 when he heard that Mr. Moody was at work in Brooklyn. Having met and worked with Mr. Moody previously, he crossed to Brooklyn and attended a Bible reading when the subject happened to be "The Holy Spirit: His Person, Offices and Work." Asked by Mr. Moody to speak, Mr. Russell made some remarks on Galatians 4, saying at one point that all believers have the Spirit of sonship, though all believers do not have the Spirit of power for service. Every believer is a child of God, being born of the Holy Spirit, but not every believer has received the filling of the Holy Spirit for service.

At this point Mr. Moody, standing by my side, struck the desk with his fist and exclaimed with vehemence: "I never saw that before! I've been troubled about that for years! I just never saw it before."

I can visualize that episode: Mr. Moody listening eagerly to Mr. Russell, catching his point, clinching it instantly in his own experience in that expressive way.

Mr. Russell says it was the following day, in the streets of New York, that Mr. Moody became conscious of a power coming upon him and flooding his whole being with an overwhelming sense of the love of God in Christ. It was God the Holy Spirit. Mr. Moody once said that during that trip East the hunger for spiritual power was ever upon him. The Chicago Fire did not dismiss or displace his yearning.

My heart was not in the work of begging. I could not appeal. I was crying all the time that God would fill me with His Spirit. Well, one day in the city of New York—ah, what a day!—I cannot describe it, I seldom refer to it, it is almost too sacred an experience to name. Paul had an experience of which he never spoke for fourteen years. I can only say God revealed Himself to me, and I had such an experience of His love that I had to ask Him to stay His hand. I went to preaching again. The sermons were not different, I did not present any new truths, and yet hundreds were converted. I would not now be placed back where I was before that blessed experience if you should give me all the world. It would be as the small dust of the balance.

continued on page 94

A FOUNDATION FOR LEADERSHIP

—— by ——

STEVE THOMPSON

All Scriptures KJV unless otherwise noted.

God chose Abraham to be the father of all who live by faith. He also chose David to begin a kingdom over which Christ Himself would rule throughout eternity. In spite of their vast leadership abilities, the Lord pointed to a simple yet profound truth as the reason that He chose both Abraham and David to be patriarchs. He chose them for their commitment to train their children.

> **And the LORD said, Shall I hide from Abraham that thing which I do;**
>
> **seeing that Abraham shall surely become a great and mighty nation, and all the nations of the earth shall be blessed in him?**
>
> *For I know [chose] him, that he will command his children and his household after him*, **and they shall keep the way of the LORD, to do justice and judgment;** *that the LORD may bring upon Abraham that which He hath spoken of him* **(Genesis 18:17-19).**

God's desire was to extend a blessing to all future generations through one man. God Himself said that He chose Abraham because He *knew* that Abraham would command his children and his descendants to follow the Lord. In fact, several versions of the Bible translate the word "know" in this verse as "chose." The Lord also clearly stated that this was necessary in order for Him to be able to fulfill His promises to Abraham. Consider also the covenant that God established with David concerning an eternal kingdom.

> **Now the days of David drew nigh that he should die; and he charged Solomon his son, saying,**
>
> **I go the way of all the earth: be thou strong therefore, and show thyself a man;**
>
> **And keep the charge of the LORD thy God, to walk in his ways, to keep his statutes, and his commandments, and his judgments, and his testimonies, as it is written in the law of Moses, that thou mayest prosper in all that thou doest, and whithersoever thou turnest thyself:**
>
> *That the LORD may continue his word which he spake concerning me, saying, If thy children take heed to*

their way, to walk before me in truth with all their heart and with all their soul, there shall not fail thee (said he) a man on the throne of Israel (**I Kings 2:1-4**).

The promises of God are always conditional upon obedience. In David's case, as well as Abraham's, because the promises were made not only to them but to succeeding generations, their fulfillment was dependent on their descendants' obedience. Therefore, it behooved both Abraham and David to train their children soundly in the ways of God.

Psalm 78:5-7 also illuminates this principle:

For [God] established a testimony in Jacob, and appointed a law in Israel, which he commanded our fathers, *that they should make them [God's dealings with Israel] known to their children:*

That the generation to come might know them, even the children which should be born; who should arise and declare them to their children:

That they might set their hope in God, and not forget the works of God, but keep his commandments.

The Scriptures bear witness to the fact that undisciplined children can bring about the end of their father's leadership. This proved true with Eli as his failure to train and discipline his sons resulted in the end of not only his leadership, but his lineage as well. Even the great prophet Samuel fell to this error of not training and disciplining his children, contributing to Israel's premature desire for a king (see I Samuel 8). If men such as Samuel were not immune to these mistakes, we would be well-advised to learn these lessons.

Loving the Lord and Living the Life

In order to train our children in the ways of the Lord, we must first love the Lord and walk in His ways. Our allegiance to Him must be supreme over every other loyalty that we have, including our families. Jesus stated this mandate when He saw the multitudes following Him.

If any man come to me, and hate not his father, and mother, and wife, and children, and brethren, and sisters, yea, and his own life also, he cannot be my disciple (Luke 14:26).

In the past decade, some contemporary proponents of the family have muddied the waters on this issue. Because some leaders may have neglected their families in a selfish pursuit of so-called "ministry," some doctrines of human origin have been created in an effort to bring balance. However, to interpret this command of Jesus we should simply consider Paul's admonition that anyone who does not provide for his own household is worse than an infidel. While we must give ourselves to the Lord first and foremost, be advised that children can be quite discerning and will often see our true motives. If we love the thrill of ministry and find ourselves using ministry as an excuse to lay aside our responsibilities to our families, they will discover us for the fakes that we are. The key to leading our families is loving God first and foremost, not our position in ministry.

In training our children, as with any type of leadership, much more is caught than taught. Although they often will hear what we say, our children will almost invariably replicate in their lives what we do with our own. Obviously then, the best leader is the one who is following the Lord. Arguably the greatest leader of the early church in terms of the greatest number of followers was Paul. It is clear that he understood where his leadership came from because he challenged the believers in Phillipi to follow him *as he followed Christ*. Do not be deceived, the servant is not greater than the master. The commitment level of those we birth and disciple is usually directly proportional to our own—how much more so our own children?

Alfred Garr, Jr., whose father was an early Pentecostal pioneer, relates that he and his siblings were awed by their father and his devotion to God. They knew that his ultimate devotion was to God. While he taught them to respect and obey the Lord with his lips, their respect for him was bought and paid for through his depth of commitment to the Lord. As a testament, each of his children went on to live exemplary lives, having tremendous influence for the Lord and the gospel. We must remember that our words will only be as effective as our lives.

The Scriptures testify that God chose Abraham and David because He knew they would *command* their children. Although this obviously included their commitment to teach, they *commanded* their generations, first and foremost, through the example of their lives. We speak of someone commanding attention, because of the strength of the testimony that their life speaks. Leaders who command generations are those who become legendary through their lives, not just their words.

It is important to understand that our children are not only blessed by our righteousness, they also suffer for our sins. Again we find this to be the case with Abraham and with David. Twice during his life Abraham told foreign kings that Sarah was his sister, not his wife, because he was afraid they would slay him in order to take her as a wife (see Genesis 12, 20). Remarkably Isaac replicated this mistake, in one of the exact same places as Abraham (see Genesis 26). It is possible that Isaac was completely unaware of his father's mistakes since both episodes occurred prior to his birth. However, what Abraham had sown in his own life eventually came forth in his son's as well.

> *"In order to train our children in the ways of the Lord, we must first love the Lord and walk in His ways."*

David also failed to escape this negative aspect of the law of sowing and reaping. After his sin of adultery with Bathsheba and the subsequent murder of Uriah, Nathan the prophet declared that evil would rise up from within David's family. Over the succeeding years his son Amnon raped his own half-sister Tamar. To revenge her, Absalom, another of David's sons, killed Amnon. Absalom later rose up against his father and was eventually killed by one of David's generals, and Adonijah, another of David's sons, also sought to take the kingdom from David. Whenever we depart from the Lord's commandments and follow our own ways, the result will be sorrow and death, not only for ourselves but for our children as well.

Lovingly Disciplining Our Children

The cornerstone and capstone of our relationship with God is the experiencing of His love. Indeed all authority ultimately is born of love. We must truly love our children in order to properly train and discipline them. Children are much more resilient than we can ever imagine; however, they are also more impressionable than we will ever know. Just as we often underestimate their ability to learn, robbing them of in-depth teaching which they could easily assimilate, we also underestimate the power of their discernment. When we administer corrective discipline, they are watching our faces and discerning our spirits. If we discipline in anger or frustration, we will communicate to them rejection instead of the loving correction which is our aim.

Ultimately whether we realize it or not, we are representing God to our children through our intent and our actions. They will eventually relate to God to some degree in the same way they learn to relate to us. Moses, Israel's greatest leader, was disqualified from leading the children of Israel into the Promised Land because he misrepresented God by his own anger, causing Israel to be afraid of God instead of trusting Him (see Numbers 20:1-13).

A practical way to avoid disciplining our children in anger and ministering rejection to them, is to consistently correct them in a timely fashion. If we base our discipline more on vision and godly principle than anger and personal frustration we will create an atmosphere of grace that enables our children to learn obedience without stifling their creativity. We must be careful that in disciplining them for disobedience we do not instill a fear of failure and keep them from attempting new endeavors. It is also of supreme importance to only discipline our children for direct disobedience to a known rule. We should simply instruct them when they use inappropriate behavior because of ignorance and never discipline them because of our own embarrassment.

> *"Ultimately whether we realize it or not, we are representing God to our children through our intent and our actions."*

Utilizing Discernment

God has made available to every parent spiritual wisdom and discernment in understanding their children. If we are lacking in this discernment personally, we have access to it through others in the body of Christ who are gifted in this area. It is extremely helpful to recognize the temperament, callings and gifts of our children at an early age. We are then able to pray for them in accordance with God's plan for their lives, as well as gear their training to fit their individual needs.

Utilizing discernment also entails understanding the enemy's strategies against our children. Satan's plan against God's work is to devour it while it is still in its infancy (see Revelation 12:4). The enemy will attack our children in subtle ways in order to cloud our understanding of their callings and temperament. We unwittingly participate in his plan against them by reacting to them as Satan would have us react, further molding their souls according to his plan.

Recently when ministering to a young child plagued with crying and fussiness for an inordinate time, a minister discerned that the child's discomfort did not come from natural physical problems. He rightly discerned that the enemy was attacking this child's body to unsettle her emotions. God revealed that had this not been recognized, the child would have experienced depression into adulthood that would have appeared to be part of her "personality." The Lord told him the child indeed had a peaceful nature and would be used of God as a peacemaker, but that the enemy was attacking her emotions as part of a long range plan against her life and calling. The parents realized that they had sided with the enemy and were wrongly labeling her in accordance with his plan. The enemy's wiles were discerned and after prayer the symptoms disappeared. These parents have now learned to fight for their child when these type of circumstances arise utilizing prayer and discernment in addition to common sense.

We see a prophetic example of this type of discernment in Scripture. Jacob refused the name that his wife chose for their son in her distress, while dying. She called him Ben-oni, which means "the son of my sorrow," but Jacob renamed him Ben-jamin, which means "the son of my right hand [authority]." By refusing to accept a negative report on his son, Jacob was waging spiritual warfare on behalf of his son. Likewise, we must discern our children's nature and calling in order to help prepare them to fulfill God's plan for their lives. They must not believe what the enemy says about them, but they must believe what God says about them. This begins with the parents. We have tremendous influence with our children and that influence can be used for the enemy or for God. We will participate in bringing the plan of one or the other to pass.

While discussing this, it is important to remember that God's power is infinitely greater than the enemy's. Satan's only power comes from deception and ignorance. When God uncovers Satan's plan the victory is already in sight. As we continue to pray for our children, God will clearly reveal His plan for their lives and expose any scheme of the enemy. The Scripture says that their angels are constantly beholding the face of our Heavenly Father. They are constantly being guarded by angels, but we must fulfill our responsibilities also.

"As we continue to pray for our children, God will clearly reveal His plan for their lives and expose any scheme of the enemy."

Discerning the calling of our children is also important. Some children have certain idiosyncracies that may reflect their spiritual calling. This is often the case with children whom God has called prophetically. When parents do not understand this, these children can experience a great amount of early rejection, again molding their souls in accordance with the enemy's plan. Rejection is the curse of those called prophetically and if it gains an early entrance, it can produce serious problems later in life.

Through proper wisdom and discernment we can steer our children into proper fields of study and discipline to prepare them for their purpose and to protect them from the weaknesses inherent in their temperaments. Regardless of how well any of us have done to date, in training our children, let us appropriate God's mercy in the areas where we have failed and His grace to begin succeeding in these same areas.

Deliverance Through Discipline

Young children do not automatically understand the appropriate way to think, feel or respond to circumstances in life. On the contrary, they usually are prone to selfishness, rebellion, anger, self-pity and other improper emotions. If negative emotions are not corrected and disciplined over time the enemy will not only build strongholds in their souls, he will seek to afflict them with sicknesses, using these emotions as a doorway. For example, self-pity can be a doorway for sicknesses such as asthma, or other ailments. Self-pity stifles spiritual development, just as asthma seeks to cut off air to the body. This does not mean that all asthma is the result of self-pity, but very often it is.

Although some children can be quite discerning about others, in general they have almost no discernment relating to their own souls. A parent's discernment is the only discernment they have in this area. Many adult human problems are simply the result of uncontrolled emotions. As a child is properly disciplined, he can be delivered spiritually and his emotions can be directed in a healthy direction toward the fruit of the Spirit. This provides a foundation for them to walk in the fruit of the Spirit as they grow older.

Understanding Ownership

We must understand that our children are gifts from God, but they do not belong strictly to us, but to Him for His purposes. We are stewards of these gifts and will be held accountable for the way in which we raise them. God has called them for signs and wonders and to be His ambassadors.

Samson is a classic example of what transpires when parents do not relinquish ownership of their children. Samson's birth was announced by an angelic visitation. The angel later reappears with instructions on how to raise him. With that kind of beginning, how could they go wrong? But into adulthood it is implied that his parents did not properly discipline him. When he found a pagan woman whose physical appearance pleased him, he told his father and mother to obtain her for him. They objected at first, but quickly gave into his demands and joined him in his folly. Eventually this lead to his demise.

Samson's parents allowed him to disobey God's commandments because they did not understand ownership. If we really understood that we were raising our children for God Himself, whose voice would we listen to? His or our children's? King David himself failed to discipline two of his sons. Both of these eventually rose up against him and sought to take his kingdom. David never questioned or corrected his son Adonijah (see I Kings 1:5-6), or his brother Absalom. Solomon, on the other hand, spoke in Proverbs of the instruction he had received from his parents.

The Samson syndrome can easily be related to by those whose children have unique callings on their life. It is understandable when a child's destiny is foretold in such a way as Samson's that we could idolize that child and fail to discipline him. However, if we properly fear God, we will take seriously His command to train our children. If God has trusted us with something as precious as a child destined to impact history, we should follow His guidelines in training them.

Samuel, whose life overlapped Samson's by twenty years, is a classic example of a child whose parents understood ownership. Consider his beginnings. His birth was special, but without the fanfare surrounding Samson's. His parents completely released Samuel to the Lord and trained him without regard to their own wishes, even to the point of giving him to Eli the priest to raise. Samuel eventually became a mighty prophet in Israel, ushering in the Davidic kingdom. The differences in Samuel's and Samson's characters, success and failure are tied, in part, to parental ownership. We must release our children to God and raise them appropriately—according to His directions.

Playing with Your Children

One devastating problem in our culture has been our tendency to overburden the souls of young children with the problems of our adult world, robbing them of their childhood innocence. Just as a baby needs a balanced physical diet in order to develop properly, our children should have an appropriate emotional diet as they are developing as well. This includes not only a tremendous amount of love and attention, but significant amounts of playtime for them to develop properly.

While many children in our society could stand more discipline, greater expectations from their parents and more challenges to stimulate them, they also need as desperately to play *with their parents*. In the church, many of our austere ways of relating to our children arise from our misunderstandings of God and His ways. God Himself plays with His children. He commanded the nation of Israel to keep three mandatory parties (feasts) each year—Passover, Pentecost and Tabernacles. Most Christians understand a God who commands us to fast, but not One who commands us to hold feasts.

An old saying states that "all work and no play makes Jack a dull boy." Not dull in the sense of boring, but dull as *Webster's* defines it: "mentally slow, slow in perception, lacking zest in vivacity, slow in action, lacking in intensity." To be sharp, our children must get a sufficient amount of play. Play is an important part of not only training our children, but the life of any healthy person. What we call recreation is really re-creation. Our souls need to be disengaged at times to recuperate just as our bodies do. How much more do young and tender souls need the freedom and enjoyment of playing with their parents? In all of our zeal to raise them for God and His purposes, we must remember that they are still children.

Encouragement for the Journey

Raising godly children is definitely not the impossible task that many have proposed and preached. It is demanding, however, especially to a generation that is as self-centered as ours. Our children have tremendous potential to impact the nations for God and His righteousness. If we will give ourselves to the task of training them in the Lord, He will reap a bountiful harvest in time. Consider the following lineage of Jonathan Edwards as reported by Leonard Ravenhill in his book, *Sodom Had No Bible*. Edwards was not only a gifted leader, he also gave himself to the process of training his children (p. 155).

> *"Our children have tremendous potential to impact the nations for God and His righteousness."*

An investigation was made of 1,394 known descendants of Jonathan Edwards of which 13 became college presidents, 65 college professors, 3 United States senators, 30 judges, 100 lawyers, 60 physicians, 75 army and navy officers, 100 preachers and missionaries, 60 authors of prominence, one a vice-president of the United States, 80 became public officials in other capacities, 295 college graduates, among whom who were governors of states and ministers to foreign countries.

Let us draw fresh inspiration to follow the Lord with abandonment and consecrate ourselves anew to train and disciple our children in the way they should go. When they are old they will not depart from it (see Proverbs 22:6). ■

Steve Thompson is the vice president of MorningStar Publications, and pastor of Hartsville Community Fellowship. He also serves on the MorningStar Ministry Team. He and his wife Angie have one son, Jon and one daughter, Moriah. They reside in Charlotte.

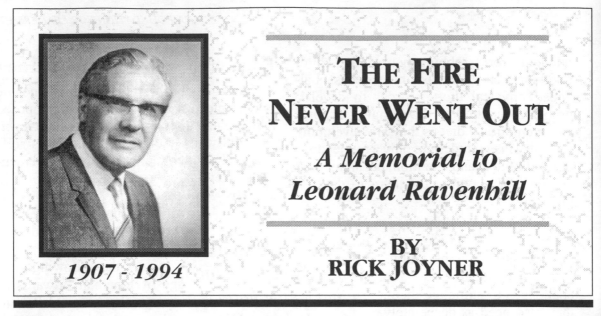

THE FIRE NEVER WENT OUT

A Memorial to Leonard Ravenhill

BY RICK JOYNER

1907 - 1994

Leonard Ravenhill died Sunday, November 27, 1994. He is survived by his wife Martha and their three sons; Paul and David, who are themselves in the ministry, and Phillip, who is a teacher. Leonard Ravenhill was born in 1907 in Leeds, Yorkshire, England. He trained at Cliff College, where it became evident that he had a special calling on his life. He went on to become one of England's foremost outdoor evangelists. During the war years his meetings drew traffic jamming crowds across Britain. Great numbers of his converts also entered the ministry. As an author his books captured and stirred a new generation to fearless, uncompromising devotion to the Lord. *Why Revival Tarries* was almost immediately considered a classic. His other books then came from his pen like spiritual tidal waves, smashing all spiritual strongholds that were built on sand.

I first met Leonard Ravenhill when he came into a meeting where I was speaking in Palestine, Texas. I did not know who he was but the Holy Spirit spoke to me and said that he was a "Simeon," who had waited long for the consolation of God's people (see Luke 2:25-35). I was told to tell him that he would be allowed to see the last day ministry in its infancy, just as Simeon in the Bible was able to hold the infant Jesus. From then on I never spent time with Brother Leonard without being profoundly impacted and challenged. I am sure that for as long as I am here, whenever I think of the great prophetic men that I have been blessed to know, he will be one of the first to come to mind.

Until the great judgment day we will never know the full extent of his impact on these times, but it is unquestionably vast. Martha Ravenhill, the Irish nurse he married in 1939, testified that his great fire never went out. Until the end he would continue to get up in the middle of the night to pray for hours for the Lord to send the revival he so desired to see.

Leonard Ravenhill will be sorely missed, but I am sure that he is quite at home in the midst of the great company of witnesses who have all earned the right to behold these times. His writings will no doubt live on, and will continue to direct many to their great destiny. He ran well, and finished his course with honor, leaving a very high standard for all who are likewise running for that imperishable wreath. ■

A Tribute To A Godly Dad

by David Ravenhill

I knew a man who gave his life,
    To see revival fire.
He prayed by day, he prayed by night,
    To birth this one desire.

He had but one obsession,
    To see a glorious bride
Arrayed in spotless purity,
    Brought to her bridegroom's side.

His power while in the pulpit
    Was matched by very few,
And yet, he loved the closet
    There with the God he knew.

While others strove for man's applause
    For fortune and for fame,
He had but one ambition
    To exalt his Master's name.

For eighty-seven years
    He lived just for eternity,
A man of faith and wisdom,
    And true humility.

He knew one day he'd have to stand,
    Before God's Judgment Seat,
And so he ran to win the prize,
    His mission to complete.

The fortune that he left behind
    Was not in stocks or gold,
But lives transformed and challenged
    Their stories yet untold.

There is no greater privilege
    Than this that I have had
Of knowing this great man of God
    And having him as DAD.

THE WATCHMAN MINISTRY continued from page 76

The Lord's correction of this one woman resulted in the entire city being opened to the gospel. This probably set the stage for Philip's later visit and the remarkable revival in that region. Whenever we bring correction, we must remember that we are correcting someone else's children—the Lord's!

The Old Covenant prophets often brought correction harshly, but they were a reflection of the covenant under which they operated— the Law, which was harsh and unyielding. We are under the age of grace, and the New Covenant prophet should reflect the nature under which he is operating. As the Lord gave us many examples, correction now comes with grace, which is both the forgiveness and the empowering to be freed from sin. We must always minister with the truth that sets people free. ■

A COUNTRY LAD BECOMES A WORLD POWER continued from page 84

Unquestionably something supernatural happened that day analogous to the marvels of the Day of Pentecost for the apostles and others, as stated in Acts 2. It was a pivotal experience that explains the remarkable change that began and matured in Mr. Moody. His personal character gained an elevation that he never lost. The Bible became a new book to him under the revealing light of God, establishing his convictions and giving him that vivid realization of things divine. As with Paul, God revealed His Son in Mr. Moody that he might preach Him among nations. The great British campaign followed the next year. His singular power in preaching, which baffled both friendly and hostile critics on the merely human level, kept its high plane to his dying day. But be used to say: "We are leaky vessels, and must take pains to have grace replenished daily."

It was my privilege to know Mr. Moody intimately, and I see in his Pentecost adequate explanation of his Christlike character and power. The seven years I was with him I never saw him do an ignoble deed, never heard him speak a mean or unkind word, never perceived in him selfish ambition or self-seeking.

I have heard of an address he gave at the College Student Conference at Northfield in 1893 when he divided his life into three definite periods: a period of nature (before conversion), a period of grace (after conversion), and a period of Power (after his filling with God the Holy Spirit).

Of course, Mr. Moody was not unique in this Pentecostal experience. Many another can testify to the same blessed fact, each in his or her own definite way, even though they were not lifted to the eminence and usefulness that Mr. Moody attained under God. An individual Pentecost is the prerogative of every believer. ■